Celtic
Cauldron

Celtic Cauldron

RITUALS for SELF-CARE
and MANIFESTATION

NICOLA McINTOSH

ROCKPOOL

A Rockpool book
PO Box 252
Summer Hill
NSW 2130
Australia

rockpoolpublishing.com
Follow us! rockpoolpublishing
Tag your images with #rockpoolpublishing

ISBN: 9781922785701

Published in 2024 by Rockpool Publishing
Copyright text and artwork © Nicola McIntosh 2024
Copyright photographs © Sabine Bannard 2024
Copyright design © Rockpool Publishing 2024

Design and typesetting by Sara Lindberg, Rockpool Publishing
Edited by Lisa Macken

Note: an Australian, Canadian and South African cup measurement
is 250 ml, while a US cup measurement is 240 ml or 8.45 imperial
fluid ounces. The difference is slight, and as long as you use the same
cup to measure your ingredients for the recipes in the following
pages the proportions will work out.

It is critical to correctly identify any plants you are using as there
are lookalikes. Also, when using any herb always check with your
medical practitioner that it is appropriate for you, especially if you
are pregnant, breastfeeding or have allergies or a medical condition
and/or are taking prescription drugs.

Printed and bound in China
10 9 8 7 6 5 4 3 2 1

REMEMBER:

YOU
ARE
THE
MAGICK

Contents

Introduction

I have been drawn to the imagery of cauldrons my whole life. My favourite novel in primary school was called *The Black Cauldron*, and it comes as no surprise that I found this path when I look back at the cover now: Celtic knotwork surrounding a black cauldron with three witches on the front. I don't know what keeps bringing me back to cauldrons, but I love them. Maybe it is the mystery and magick of them, maybe it is a remembrance or a connection from past lives, but I knew I had to explore it further. I didn't want mine to just be a pretty object in my home or on my altar; I wanted to work with it and create from it. I wanted to explore the possibilities of what it represents and how we can utilise these qualities in our modern day-to-day lives.

Although cauldrons have been adopted in many pagan practices such as witchcraft and wicca, their history dates back hundreds of years before that. The Celts didn't have a name for witches or shamans, because what we term 'magick' today was something that was well entrenched in daily life and not seen as unusual. Shamans were called *walkers between the worlds*. The Druids also worked with the natural world, which we view now as being magickal.

It was when the witch hunts began in the Middle Ages that this way of life unfortunately became hidden and somewhat forgotten for fear of persecution. Today there is such a stigma and romanticised view of what a witch or shaman is that I feel it's time to return an earth-centred craft to the forefront. We no longer live with the fear of persecution for practising our beliefs, so why should we hide our spiritual sides away from view? We cannot separate these aspects of ourselves, and part of the dis-ease in Western society is because of this separation. We are not living the way nature intended.

Stephen Harrod Buhner in his book *Sacred Plant Medicine* (Raven Press, 2001) uses the term 'Earth-Centered spirituality'. I love this term, as so many practices can fall under this umbrella. There has been such an explosion of knowledge thanks to the internet and technology, along with extensive migration and travel, that we are now easily able to learn about different cultural beliefs, practices, religions, rituals, foods, history and spiritual beliefs. We are thus learning multiple modalities and becoming multifaceted human beings. We no longer fit one hat or one job description and when you go to someone's social media profile they generally have a list of what they do because they don't fit into one job title anymore. It makes sense then, that we stop trying to fit into one spiritual label and start streamlining earth-centred spiritual practices into our daily lives, like many indigenous cultures worldwide still do.

The reality from my perspective is there is one energy manifesting itself in many ways that has been labelled many different things and most religions and spiritual practices have similar themes. We are all working towards the same goals, just by different definitions. Now is the time we can all come together for a common purpose. Now is the time to work together.

I understand that we are all trying to make a living and marketing is based around finding the next best thing, the next new label or fad, the new shiny toy, the new healing modality or the new spiritual practice that is better than all the others. We are getting lost in all the noise of new courses to learn, new books to read, new ways of doing things and we are getting lost in the overwhelm of choice. We are looking for one direction, but there are so many paths. We don't know who to believe, who to trust or who to follow, which is why creating your own daily rituals is so important. Do the simple things to ground yourself: bring yourself into the present, find a way to centre yourself and take time out from the hustle and bustle, because this is where you find your answers and direction. It's time to put down the books (except this one, of course) and do the practice. Only then will you find what you are looking for.

Our spiritual, daily rituals and self-care routines are ever-increasingly important in the current times. Helping one another and lifting others up is another priority. Working together to look at sustainable practices and caring for the earth is just as important. If we were to all do this together, imagine what we could achieve.

How does all this relate to the cauldron? We do live in an age where the laws of attraction and manifestation are understood, which thankfully has become somewhat mainstream. Rituals of any form serve the purpose of shifting our focus and intention on what we wish to draw into our lives. You see, we are the creators of our reality; therefore, when we understand how this works we can set about creating a more positive flow in our lives and make our dreams a reality.

Do we really need a cauldron? The short answer is 'No.' The longer answer is this: ritual is an incredibly powerful practice. Bringing ritual into our daily life can bring about incredible changes. To begin to understand how something works it is good to have a recipe to follow because it educates us on how to construct things, and then when we are confident we can follow the recipe, we can substitute things and make our own recipes. When we understand how the laws of nature and manifestation really work we understand we don't need the label either; we connect wholly with nature and just 'are'. This is where the true magick reveals itself: you no longer feel as though you are acting out something fantastical, because you realise you truly are manifesting your world into being. The other upside is you finally get to use that cauldron you've been longing to use, and that in itself becomes a magickal object imbued with your energy and intentions.

The intention of this book is to act as a guide to making beautiful creations that will aid you in creating a deeper connection with the natural world and manifest real change in your life. To achieve that purpose we will work with plant and crystal spirits and many everyday household supplies because it's about learning to work with what you have and what is around you in your immediate environment, just as your ancestors did. Let your intuition guide you, and if you don't have some of the ingredients in the recipes then intuitively substitute them with something else or look up the extensive herb and crystal reference section in appendixes I and II. You can make a recipe unique to your culture, your country and your environment and spiritual practices. This is the Celtic way.

In these pages I offer my modern take on how we can work with the natural world, honour their energies and ask for their help in manifesting change within ourselves and our world. It's a book with new ideas and ways of thinking, so take what feels right and adapt what you want. It's time to create new practices that reflect the modern age we live in. Our spiritual practices need to resonate with us, because if we feel silly doing them then they won't have the effect we are looking for. What we must remember is that intention is key, and if we feel in alignment with the energies we are working with and the practices we are doing then that is all that matters.

Instead of giving you pages and pages of recipes with all manner of ingredients that you might not have, I have instead given you instructions on how to make each item and suggested herbs or plants that would be suitable options. However, in this book I wish to show you how to incorporate your own herbs and plants into your cauldron and self-care rituals and ceremonies so they become something unique to you and your culture – something that resonates with you and gives you a deeper connection with the plant world around you, which will help in manifesting your dreams and living a fulfilling life. If you can grow your own herbs even better, because this will reduce your impact on the earth and the environment and will also allow you to gain a deeper connection with the plants themselves as you watch them go through their seasons and changes. Just the act of caring for a plant will bring you closer connection to it.

WHO WERE THE CELTS?

Many people associate the Celtic people with coming from Ireland, England, Wales and Scotland. The Celts, in fact, were spread throughout Europe and may have originated from Austria. Their distinctive art style has lasted throughout the ages and carries with it great meaning in itself, such as the never-ending and intertwining knotwork that is symbolic of there being no beginning or end and that everything is connected.

The Celts were a complex race of people. Both women and men were fierce warriors who prided themselves on grooming, hygiene and incredible artisan skills and had a deep understanding of nature's cycles and the importance of working with nature, which is evident in their artwork, myths and legends. Being a Celt does not mean you need to have lineage from there, as it was more of a lifestyle than a religion or race from a particular location. Many were travellers, and with them they took the Celtic ways for others to adopt as they saw fit. You might feel a calling to the Celtic ways and if you do, trust your gut, follow your intuition and discover the connection you have been longing for.

CHAPTER 1

The history of the cauldron

The cauldron was not an invention of the Celts: it had been around for possibly thousands of years before them. However, it seems that the Celtic civilisation gave great importance to their cauldrons. Many have been unearthed in Ireland, Wales and Scotland, unused and in many cases in burial sites. Not only did the Celts make them extremely large for cooking huge feasts, they seem to have used them for spiritual practices and other practices that are no longer known. The cauldrons were made from bronze, copper or iron depending on what era they were from.

The cauldron was an invaluable item in every home, as it was a device in which to cook, clean, dye fabrics and store items. In fact, not having one was foreign. As modern-day conveniences such as ovens made their way into homes the cauldron began to lose its fundamental use. We now use plastic buckets and laundry sinks for many things, and the cauldron is viewed by many as a witch's tool and has been over-commercialised as such.

GUNDESTRUP CAULDRON

The Gundestrup cauldron, the most famous cauldron ever discovered to date, is a 97 per cent pure silver bowl that dates back to approximately the 2nd or 1st century BCE. Measuring almost 70 cm (28 in) in diameter and 42 cm (17 in) in height, it was found buried and in pieces. Carefully reconstructed, it still holds much debate as to its origins, although it appears to have arrived in Denmark via trade or perhaps as a gift or stolen goods.

One section of the relief artwork depicting Cernunnos.

The Gundestrup cauldron is highly decorative, with relief pictures around the entire piece created through a process called repoussé. It originally had some gold gilding and glass inserts in some of the eyes on it. Silver was not a common material for a cauldron to be made from and the Celts did not normally use it; however, skilled artisans residing in Thrace, or modern-day Bulgaria, used these handcrafting skills. The art is known to be Celtic and depicts Celtic gods, themes, animals and plants. There are also exotic, mythical animals, which may suggest that the makers or people who had it made likely travelled. Scholars continue to debate and may never know the true meanings of the art, but wherever it came from it was a prized possession.

The most well-known image on the cauldron is that of the horned figure, who is recognised as Cernunnos, the horned god in Celtic mythology. It is a seated man with antler horns, holding a serpent in one hand and a torc or Celtic necklace in the other, as well as wearing a torc around his neck. He is surrounded by animals and plants, including a stag. Cernunnos was the lord of the animals, and the two torcs represent abundance and wealth.

BATTERSEA CAULDRON AND CHISELDON CAULDRONS

The Battersea cauldron, which dates from 800 to 700 BCE and is thus in excess of 2,700 years old, was discovered in the Thames riverbed in 1861. Constructed from riveted bronze sheets, it features two handles on top and is in extremely good condition for its age. The Battersea cauldron currently resides in the British Museum.

The Chiseldon cauldrons from the 4th or 3rd century BCE are a group of 17 Iron Age cauldrons, some with Celtic art, that were found at a site in Chiseldon in south-west England. This is the largest complete cauldron find from Iron Age Europe to date. The cauldrons had been buried with some face up and some face down, while one of the cauldrons was purposely damaged before being buried in the circular pit. There were also two cow skulls placed in the south part of the pit. It is important to note that they were complicated to manufacture and sophisticated techniques were used.

The Chiseldon cauldrons currently reside in the British Museum. Extensive information on this find can be found in *A Celtic Feast: The Iron Age Cauldrons from Chiseldon, Wiltshire* by Alexandra Baldwin and Jody Joy (Research Publication 203 by the British Museum, 2017).

Battersea cauldron.

GLENFIELD PARK CAULDRONS

Bordering the lands where the Chiseldon cauldrons were found, another 11 cauldrons were discovered in a similar manner: they were buried in a circular pit facing both up and down, along with other items of importance such as jewellery. It is thought the finds were buried over a lengthy period of time and may have been linked to some sort of ceremonial centre.

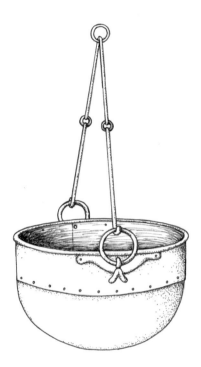

Replica of a Chiseldon cauldron that resides at Chiseldon Village Museum.

Archaeologists believe that large feasts were made in many of the ancient cauldrons that have been found and have discovered evidence of plant and meat material inside them as well as signs of being repaired, indicating they were in use for some time. Their use in social gatherings seemed to make them powerful objects.

THE THREE CAULDRONS

One thing I find interesting is the concept of the three cauldrons as energy centres within the body. It is mentioned in early literature and in a seventh-century Irish poem called 'Cauldron of Poesy'. These vessels were known as the cauldrons of knowledge, vocation and warmth. There is some debate over the information in the poem, about whether it relates specifically to where all poetry or inspiration

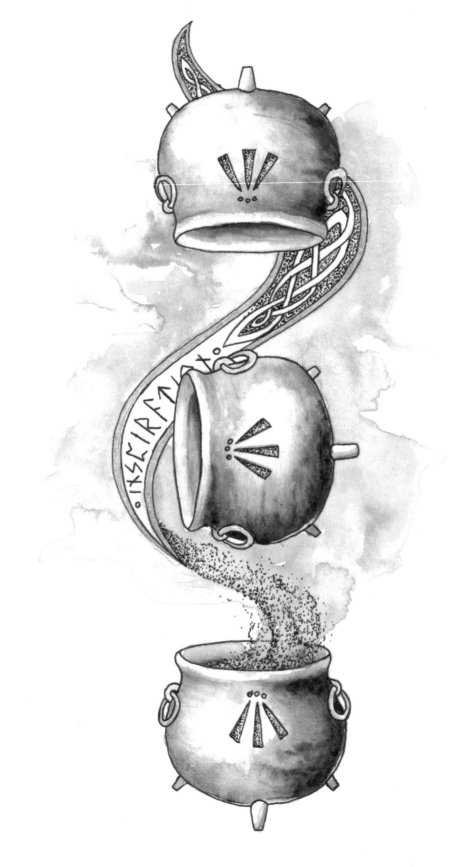

flows from or a spiritual quest that must be undertaken. Whichever way you decide to interpret it, the messages are clear and logical:

* knowledge/wisdom/inspiration: represents the upper world/sky/future, located at or on the head
* vocation/motion: represents the middle world/land/present, located in the chest
* warmth/incubation: represents the lower world/land/past.

According to the poem, the cauldrons are situated in the following manner: the lower is standing upright, the middle on its side and the upper upside down. The position of the cauldrons may change, and the poet refers to the positions with regards to 'no knowledge, half knowledge and full knowledge'. The quest is to fill the cauldrons and have them all standing upright, akin to filling your cup. Was the cauldron used as a metaphor at the time because of its important uses in the household, making it a very relatable subject? The cauldron is also known as being feminine and relating to the womb, wherein which life is created.

CAULDRONS OF MYTHOLOGY

There is mention of magickal cauldrons in early mediaeval literature from Ireland and Wales that needs to be explored. When working with gods and goddesses it can be a little confusing at first to know what exactly we are working with. Are the myths and legends just stories? Are they intellectual concepts arranged into stories to teach us something or were they arranged into stories to save the information from being destroyed or lost? Before civilisation had the ability to read and write they drew pictures or handed down their knowledge via stories and songs. Are these stories from a time when advanced civilisations were perceived to have god-like abilities, or are they a manifestation of an energy that can be called upon that shows itself in the only way it knows how to communicate effectively? Do they reside in another realm on the edge of our physical, dense reality? Maybe it is a group consciousness that wills the energy into being, purely by the mere belief that it exists. Whatever way you choose to believe, know that when you call upon their energy, you are calling in the aspects they are known for and the vibrational energy that resides behind their form.

CAULDRON OF REBIRTH

The Pair Dadeni, or the Cauldron of Rebirth, belonging to Brân the Blessed was known to revive dead warriors, although they would not be able to speak afterwards.

DAGDA'S CAULDRON

Dagda's cauldron is also a famous magickal cauldron. The Tuatha Dé Danann (pronounced *tooah day danahn*) were a tribe of people with god-like abilities who arrived in Ireland and ruled over it more than 4,000 years ago. With them they brought four treasures from their four cities: the Sword of Nuada, the Spear of Lugh, the Lia Fáil or the Stone of Destiny and the Cauldron of Dagda. 'Dagda', meaning the 'good god', was the god of the Tuatha Dé Danann and was said to have magickal powers and incredible knowledge. He possessed three treasures of great power: a club that killed with one blow and could revive with the opposite end, a living harp that could control the emotions of men and the seasons, and a famous bronze cauldron, the Undry or Cauldron of Plenty. No matter how many people ate from the cauldron, no one left without being satisfied. This is yet another symbol of regeneration and rebirth.

CERRIDWEN'S CAULDRON

The Welsh goddess Cerridwen was known for her cauldron of knowledge, transformation and rebirth, her connection with Taliesin and her knowledge of herbs and magick. The tale relates that Cerridwen had a very ugly son, so she decided to make a brew in her cauldron that would bestow upon him great knowledge so he would not become an outcast. She hired Gwion Bach to help with the stirring of the brew for a year and a day, and at the end of that time he accidentally got

three drops of the brew on his hand that he immediately sucked off. Instantly he was given the knowledge of the world, which should have gone to Cerridwen's son. She flew into a rage and chased Gwion, who transformed into a hare and ran away. Cerridwen shapeshifted into a greyhound and chased the hare, but the hare ran with all its might and jumped into a river. He became a salmon and swam down the river, so Cerridwen shapeshifted again but this time into an otter. The otter chased the salmon until the salmon shot out of the water and changed into a small wren and flew away. Cerridwen sped after him, changing into a hawk.

The chase continued until Cerridwen was about to catch Gwion, when he changed into a single grain of wheat and dropped out of the sky into a pile of wheat at a farm. Cerridwen turned into a hen, started eating the grain and ate Gwion, becoming pregnant with him. When she gave birth to him she intended to kill him, but upon seeing his beautiful face she fell in love. However, she knew she must get rid of the baby so she put him inside a skin belly and placed him in the mystical waters between the worlds until he was found by Elffin, who later became his loyal servant. He grew up and became the great Taliesin.

Cerridwen was a *swyn*, which was the closest Welsh word for what we term a 'witch' today, before that English word was ever bestowed on anyone for the purposes of the witch hunts. Her re-emergence in modern times has brought her to the forefront once again, and the meaning of her cauldron remains one of transformation, knowledge and rebirth. There is thought that the cauldron is Cerridwen and thus becomes a cauldron of inspiration, a place to bring together everything needed to create and inspire. The cauldron is said to contain the Awen or be the cup of Awen, or the Cauldron of Inspiration. The Welsh word 'Awen' means 'inspiration' or 'essence' and is the inspiration of poets and creative artists.

Chapter 2

Modern applications and manifestation

I f the witch hunts had not taken place and the Celts and Druids had been left to continue their crafts and practices, can you imagine how advanced their teachings would be today? Sometimes we get a little fixated on how things were practised and think we need to do them the same way in this day and age, but when you think about how society has changed with the internet, travel and multiculturalism, what other practices do you think they would have added into their day-to-day lives? Would they be using all manner of crystals and herbs not native to their area or would they continue to utilise what was in their immediate environment?

Maybe the teachings of the Celts and Druids would be about how to cultivate their practices within your environment no matter where you live or what culture you are from. Everything evolves, and so too do we need to let our beliefs and practices evolve and there is nothing wrong with cherry picking from other religions and practices. I believe in reincarnation, and because of this fact my belief says that we may have experienced living the lives of many different people on earth. We may have been a witch in the UK or America, a Native American, an Aboriginal of

Australia or a Caucasian in Western society. We use these lifetimes to learn different lessons and thus gain a better understanding of one another. This may also be why we are drawn to certain cultures: we could have been one of them in a previous life. We are all spiritual beings having human experiences on earth.

It is up to us to evolve our spiritual beliefs for this modern age and time. They will most likely change again, but at the heart of it all is the key to manifestation and creation:

What we can imagine we can create.

We can never be separated from the natural world because we *are* nature. This is where our magick lies. We are the creators and the spiritual practices focus our intent on what we wish to manifest. When we work with plant allies, crystal spirits, animal totems and all manner of natural items we create a unified field of many energies working together for a common cause, and this is indeed powerful. Never underestimate the power that resides within seemingly insignificant objects. The more we work with them the more energy they acquire, until you can sense the magick they hold.

The rituals we create can be as simple or elaborate as we choose. As we keep up with the demands of everyday life we can find ourselves time poor or lacking the energy we wish we could put into doing more elaborate rituals, so inevitably don't do any at all. The best way to bring something new into your life is in small amounts: 15 minutes a day, every second day or even once a week is enough, but you need to make it a regular practice so it becomes a habit. It needs to have meaning and it needs to leave you feeling connected and empowered. Make it your ritual of self-care and spiritual connection. If you do this for 15 minutes a day before you start your day you will notice an incredible difference.

The point of this book is to get you using your cauldron and making ritual a daily practice in your life to help you connect with spirit and manifest your dreams. Make it unique to you; don't feel as though you have to follow what everyone else is doing. There is no right or wrong way so trust your intuition, and most of all have fun.

The other key point I need to mention is to remember that *you are the magick*. Just by wishing something so doesn't make it happen. It is your intention, followed by your action, that will manifest what you desire. When we work on ourselves things may come up that can be difficult to deal with, but that is where the gift is. When we work through obstacles we change ourselves and allow stagnant and lower-vibrational energy to move, which means a higher vibration flows within us. In order to manifest what we want we must be a vibrational match to it.

When we cast out our intentions through ritual and ceremony we are essentially asking for the blocks that stand in the way of reaching our goals to be removed. It is you who must deal with them, and when you finally become a vibrational match you will receive what you asked for. You might not receive it in the manner in which you thought it would arrive, but upon inspection it will be exactly what you asked for and sometimes everything you didn't know you needed.

CHOOSING A CAULDRON

There are many kinds of cauldrons you can purchase in various places, but not all are the same. You might like to choose a few different ones for different applications or find one that will suit them all. The most important thing to note is that if you intend to use your cauldron for making anything to be ingested or placed on the skin it needs to be food safe. Sometimes this is difficult to determine, so if you are unsure find something you know is definitely safe.

Spirituality for me means choosing everything responsibly, ethically and sustainably. Please do not add to the plastic problem by purchasing or making cauldrons that are plastic, resin or other materials that are damaging to the environment. Always keep in mind that when you are gone your cauldron will still remain: do you want it to be litter on the earth, or something that can be handed down and used by generations to come? When we follow an earth-centred approach to spirituality you will be challenged by finding ways of creating products that are good for the environment and will hold positive vibrations. I love op-shop finds or second-hand goods for my cauldrons, as well as making my own ceramic ones. Why not support a local potter?

Below are listed some of the materials or vessels that can be used as cauldrons.

Cast-iron cauldrons.

Cast iron. If cared for properly cast iron can last hundreds of years and is safe for just about everything. Cast-iron cauldrons come in a range of styles, from the small ones you find in spiritual stores to camp ovens at camping stores and Dutch ovens from kitchen supply stores. Another one you can find is a 'potjie' (pronounced *poi key*), a South African cooking pot. Also check Asian grocery stores, as they usually have some awesome cast-iron pots and stands for an affordable price and look for shabu and sukiyaki pots and hibachi stoves. Asian cultures still cook many meals via these methods and I've found a whole other world of potential cauldrons down this avenue that are perfect!

If you get a cauldron that you know is used for cooking food then you know it will be safe to use for all of your recipes.

> *Note: if you buy a cast-iron cauldron that has been painted (they should be naturally black) do not use it for anything you will heat, eat or put on your skin as you won't know what the paint is and it could potentially be toxic.*

Fondue pot. Fondue pots are fantastic to use as modern-day cauldrons and were very popular in the 1970s. You can find cast-iron, enamel, steel and copper ones. The benefit of these is that they already come with a stand and burner underneath, so they are great to use outside or take with you to ritual places and you know they are food safe. You can also find electric fondue pots, which are a great option if you don't want to use a naked flame. Be careful with vintage enamel pots and especially if they are chipped or old, as some have been known to be toxic.

Fondue cauldron.

Ceramic. Ceramic cauldrons are a favourite of mine and I love to sip my tea or mushroom brew from a cauldron mug. Ceramic cauldrons should be able to take the heat of a flame but you should always check that your vessel can stand the heat. If you buy from a potter they will be able to tell you. You will also need to know whether the glaze they use is food safe if you are going to ingest anything made in your cauldron.

Ceramic cauldron.

Tea stove and cauldron.

Teaware. The Chinese are well known for their teaware, so finding a tea stove online is not hard: once you start looking it's like going down a rabbit hole! These are used for brewing tea and making meals, so you might like to get one if you drink or boil a lot of herbs or teas.

Stainless steel or copper. You can find stainless-steel or copper cauldrons, bowls, pots and pans that can tolerate heat, but also remember you can have practically any vessel for the many cauldron uses that don't require any heat.

Note: copper cauldrons and pans can only be used to heat if they are lined with another metal, as copper can leach into your food and liquids. Stainless-steel lined ones are best.

Copper doesn't require high heat as it distributes the heat around the vessel equally, making them great to cook with. Copper cauldrons with no lining can be used to store room-temperature water, but do not leave it in there for extended periods of time. Some copper does leach into the water, although in safe doses that are actually good for you as they have anti-bacterial qualities, which keeps your water fresh for drinking. Copper vessels were originally used for this purpose.

Copper cauldrons.

Tempered glass. There are so many tempered-glass products these days that come in a range from Pyrex jugs to casserole dishes that make suitable cauldrons. They may not feel as magickal as a normal cauldron but they will not leach or absorb anything, making them very practical for an array of applications.

Tempered-glass products.

The important thing to note is to not get too caught up in what your cauldron looks like. Just know that it is a tool and it is capable of creating magickal products!

CAULDRON CARE

Cast-iron cauldrons need to be seasoned and prepped before their first use, which creates a barrier on the surface so you don't get any metallic taste. It will also stop your cauldron from rusting.

When cleaning and seasoning cast iron the number one rule is to not use any soap or dishwashing liquid, because it can strip the coating from the cast iron and cast iron is absorbent and can leave a soapy taste. Essentially, it won't cause any damage if you do use those products, but be sure to rinse the cauldron thoroughly and season it well. You will need to use unsaturated fat to season your cauldron, so olive or vegetable oil and shortening or lard is best. If you have a rusty cauldron you can use this method to restore it:

- Remove any debris from inside and outside the pot and/or potential coating that may be on the surface. If there is a lot of rust you may need to use steel wool, sandpaper or a steel brush. Also do this to the lid if you have one.
- Wash the pot with warm water and dry thoroughly.
- Preheat the oven to 175°C/350°F and place a tray in the bottom that is covered with foil or baking paper.
- Using a paper towel, rub the oil over the entire surface of the cauldron inside and out, including the lid.
- Turn the cauldron upside down and place it inside the pre-heated oven for 1 hour. Any excess oil will drip into the tray below. If the cauldron is too big to fit in the oven you can heat it up over a fire.
- Remove the cauldron and lid from the heat source and allow it to cool. You can remove any excess oil with paper towels as it is cooling. If it is sticky it may have too much oil on it, so you might like to reheat it again.

Never leave water or fluids in a cauldron for extended periods of time unless they are cooking: water + metal = rust. If you cook anything acidic such as tomatoes in a cast-iron pot it can gradually reduce the seasoning, so you may like to reseason it depending on how much you use it. The metallic taste will eventually leach into your food if you cook using tomatoes for any length of time. Your cauldron is now ready for use.

Copper cauldrons need to be free of the green tarnish they can acquire as it is toxic. A good natural way to remove the tarnish or to clean the cauldron is to use a mix of lemon juice and bicarbonate of soda. Just mix a small amount together and rub with a clean cloth then rinse with warm water. You can also use soap to clean copper.

Ceramic cauldrons: if you are using an unglazed ceramic pot never clean the inside with soap and water. Just rinse it out straight after use with warm water as the ceramic can absorb the soap. For all other pots that are glazed you can use soap and water but make sure you give it a really good rinse out afterwards, and you can also use a paste of bicarbonate of soda and water if it needs a little scrub.

* * *

Spiritual preparation is always recommended when you acquire a new cauldron. It can be as simple as making space for it on your altar and verbally declaring that you now dedicate your cauldron to manifesting your desires or for magickal workings. You could also do something more elaborate by creating a ritual around your cauldron by smudging and placing offerings in it. Make it yours; there is no right or wrong way. Intent is always key.

Before starting I must address **the safety of using a cauldron with a heat source**. These vessels get *extremely* hot, especially cast-iron ones. Please have a tea towel or pot mitt handy along with a trivet or board to place the lid on if it is hot.

If you are using a fondue-type of vessel that has a container underneath filled with methylated spirits, ensure it has a lid to put it out when you're finished. *Do not* try to blow the flame out as you will spread the flame. These vessels usually have little vents you can close that eventually starve the flame of oxygen and go out. If you are worried, have a fire blanket, extinguisher or sand close by.

If you are using your cauldron outside ensure there are no fire bans in your area or anything flammable nearby.

Please *always* use caution and be safe. It is very easy to panic in a situation with fire, so prevention is key.

With your cauldron now ready, it's time to start creating!

CHAPTER 3

CREATING
A RITUAL

R ituals have been around for aeons and have been used extensively worldwide by all civilisations. There is nothing to fear through ritual and you don't have to belong to any faith at all, because a ritual is simply a practice that brings us into the present moment and shifts our focus toward something we wish to achieve or draw into our lives. A ritual can be anything you do on a regular basis that brings you closer to spirit or nature, and it can be simple or elaborate and encompass the beliefs and items you feel drawn to. It is important to understand that you do not have to conform to any other way, because it is all about intent and it needs to feel right for you. Another way to look at ritual is calling it a ceremony. The word 'ritual' in itself can have so many connotations attached to it that 'ceremony' may sit with you better.

As with any recipe we first need an intention. What do we want to create or manifest? It might be a simple request or something much larger, but we need to be very clear on what we want to achieve. You might wish for a promotion, to find a new friend, bring peace or love into your life, create a home-based business or acquire a new car or home. You may also be looking for guidance or direction on an issue or wanting to boost your self-esteem, find your purpose or create a healthier you.

Creating a crystal-clear vision is a necessary part to understanding what you will need for your ritual.

Why? Because we want to focus on the end result and draw that to us, which will allow us to look for what might complement our intention. For instance, if we want to find love we generally associate that with pink gemstones, rose petals, softness and so on, so we go in search of the items that invoke that feeling within us. We need to become the vibration of love.

Ritual is about the summoning of energy to direct to your intention. A ritual doesn't need to be all hocus pocus and capes; it can be as simple as having a morning cuppa in your favourite seat and overlooking your garden while sitting with your cat. You are taking time out for yourself and being present with yourself, your garden and your cat. You have invited these different energies together, which creates a sense of peace and happiness within yourself. This feeling sets the energy for the day.

Rituals can literally change anything within your life. When we turn our attention inwards, we make big changes in our internal environment and our vibrations change, creating a different external environment because *we attract what we are.* This is key to manifestation: We must be in alignment with what we wish to draw into our life. In other words, we must be a vibrational match to what we wish to manifest. You can make your rituals elaborate or simple, because it is your intention and focus that are key. The ritual is the practice that helps you focus your intention and keeps you in the present moment. Sometimes less means fewer distractions and things to think about.

Another part to ritual is calling in the spirit allies you need to help you with your intention. Your spirit allies aren't looking in on you 24/7, which is why you need to call them in and say, 'Please, I need your help with . . .' When the meeting is over you thank your spirit allies and they go off to do what they need to do. I liken this part to calling everyone in for a board meeting or getting everyone on the same page for a common cause, as then the collective energy from all allies with the same intention becomes a very powerful force. If we look at everything in the natural world including specific plants, crystals and natural objects as manifestations of spirit or source energy, then we are working with this energy.

Spirit is able to see what we need better than we can, so we need to trust and surrender to the process. What we may see as an obstacle or negative situation could in fact be exactly what we need to look at differently in order to get to where we need to be. Spiritual growth is not about chocolates and roses, it's about overcoming obstacles and coming to realisations on our own and then making changes in our lives. Sometimes it takes something big and traumatic, while at other times it can be an easy shift in our understanding. We may take a few steps back and that is totally fine: if we just keep putting one foot in front of the other, eventually we will get to where we need to be. Remember that you are always where you need to be, and use that to ask yourself: 'What can I learn from this?'

THE IMPORTANCE OF SELF-CARE

Using your cauldron and ritual plays a big part in self-care. How? By bringing you into the present, slowing your body and mind down, relieving stress from your body, connecting more with your spiritual side and nature among other things. The more you take the time to create this sacred practice the more you will yearn for it.

Stress, one of the major contributors to the leading causes of death, is linked to heart disease, cancer, poor mental health, suicide, liver and lung conditions. Not only does stress raise the heart rate, it can have long-lasting effects on the nervous system. Chronic stress generates a constant adrenaline rush that can lead to adrenal exhaustion. The effect stress can have on our mental health is massive, and it causes a knock-on effect with our whole body and organs. The human body is capable of dealing with a certain amount of stress effectively, but it was never meant to withstand the long-term stress that is prevalent in modern society.

Coupled with stress is usually an inability to make time to look after ourselves and our spiritual practices. I mean, who wants to sit down and rest when there is so much to do, right? We can feel guilty for taking time out for ourselves while chores sit around begging to be done. You'd be surprised by how much you can get done when you're in a rested state and in flow.

ALTARS AND SHRINES

Many cultures throughout the world use altars and shrines. Quite simply, they are special places you put valued items of your own that won't be disturbed by anyone or anything that allow you to create a sacred space for your intention. This may be a special table or shelf you have for your favourite crystals, plants, pictures, jewellery and so on, where you go to meditate or light incense for the day. It may be your bubble that allows you to step away from the mundane world for a moment and feel a closer connection with spirit and nature.

If the idea of setting up an altar is foreign to you and you don't know if the people you live with will understand, just clear a place on your desk or drawers where you put some special items and no one will need to know it's your altar. I fully understand that altars aren't everyone's cup of tea, and you need to feel comfortable and safe creating one. At the end of the day an altar teaches you how to take time out and be present with spirit and your higher self. It is a space that allows you to just 'be'. Nature can be your altar, and the cup or bowl you eat and drink from can be your cauldron. Setting your intent is all that matters.

The wonderful thing about altars and shrines is that there are no rules and anyone from any culture or any faith can have one. Make it your own; make more than one! You can make mini altars and travel and garden ones. Once you start you'll find lots of places you can set them up, making everywhere you go sacred. Your altar will change over time, and every time you clean it you may want to remove something or add to it. Just as your energy changes, so too will the energy of your altar the more you work at it.

What sorts of things might you put on your altar? You could, for instance, place an object for each of the four elements such as: a water bowl or shell to represent water; a candle for fire; a crystal, rock or even a plant for earth; and a feather or incense to represent air. If you are into feng shui you might like to incorporate the five elements of fire, metal, wood, air and water. You could also include feathers, plants, incense burners, wands, spirit sticks, oracle and tarot cards, flowers, cauldrons, animal items to represent totem animals and pictures.

Exercise: CREATING YOUR ALTAR

For this exercise you will need to find a place either in your home or outside that you can visit every day that will not be disturbed by anyone or anything. This can be as simple as a little table, a shelf or space in your garden, or you could even make your own table or shelf from what you have around or find something at an op shop or an online marketplace you can spruce up. The more energy you put into it the more energy it will hold, so put as much of yourself into it as possible.

If you have children, let them know the importance of it being your space. This may inspire them to create their own. You could make a small altar for you all to enjoy, remembering that there are no rules except making it a sacred space that you all respect.

Tend to your altar as often as you can, ensuring it doesn't get too dirty or dusty because this represents stagnation. Any plant material that is no longer needed on your altar should be disposed of thoughtfully. Don't throw something sacred in the rubbish bin: either give it back to the earth by placing it in your compost or physically put it back in your garden to decompose. Everything you do must be done mindfully and with respect. Anything taken must be asked for, so ensure if you are taking a leaf or flower for your altar you first ask for its permission.

RITUAL CREATING

Remember, there are no rules for performing your ritual. Do you notice a common theme happening here? You are the creator, which means you can make your ritual whatever you like. When we think we can do something wrong, we shut down our right creative brain and our spiritual flow. The key points to any ritual are:

* setting your intent
* calling in your spiritual helpers and guides even if you don't know who they are

- ✳ being present and allowing yourself to feel into what you are doing as much as possible, as well as being open and receptive to what you may receive

- ✳ being respectful and treating everything as sacred, including yourself

- ✳ making sure your thoughts are about pure love and intent and that everything you do has no impact on the environment or harms anyone in any way.

What about verses, incantations and spellcasting? This needs to be a personal decision: if you feel silly doing it then don't, but if it feels natural then do. The purpose of creating a rhyme of some sort to use in ritual serves to focus your attention and intention in the present moment. It can be a mantra or even a prayer of some description. The use of sound and the spoken word also have their own power, and when there is an emotional connection to them then it can significantly add to your ceremony or ritual. Your words can be seen as the vehicle for your intent to travel on. Singing is another practice that many indigenous cultures worldwide do when in ceremony. Sound, speech and music all have their own medicine.

JOURNALLING

I have journals for literally everything, because they are invaluable and don't take much time to do but will record a wealth of information that can be referred back to. I like to keep one for each subject I might study or one to record meditations, but I always have one to put all my recipes in and this is what I recommend for doing the work in this book. You can be as detailed or brief as you like, but make sure your journal becomes a valued tool. I usually buy leather-wrapped journals with handmade paper, but I also have cheap spiral-bound books from the grocery store in small and large sizes for various things.

You essentially are creating a grimoire. If you're looking for a beautiful journal to do your work in make sure you search 'grimoire' on the internet; there is an abundance of suitable books. You might like to do yourself up a nice sheet that you print out each time you want to create a new ritual or recipe and place them in a ring binder.

Here are some suggestions for headings you can write in your journal. You don't have to complete each one, and obviously you can add your own:

RECIPE/INTENTION/RITUAL

What is my intention for this ritual?

_____

_____

_____

What product will I make?

_____

Best date and time to perform my ritual?

What moon cycle is best?

_____

Chakra colour associations

Astrological associations

Crystals I could use

Direction to be facing

Plants I could use

List of ingredients to use

_____

_____

Equipment I will need

_____

Expectations and uses

_____

_____

Incantation/affirmation/intention statement

_____

_____

_____

Directions

_____
_____
_____
_____
_____
_____
_____

Results

_____
_____
_____
_____
_____
_____

What worked

_____
_____
_____
_____

What didn't

_____
_____
_____

Notes

_____
_____
_____
_____
_____

Exercise: 30-DAY CAULDRON RITUAL

The intent of this 30-day cauldron ritual is to get you into the habit of using both your cauldron and altar, as well as starting to make the time for your spiritual practices and understand the importance they have on your body, mind and soul. You don't want it to be stressful or feel like a chore, so it's best to start off small. Everyone can find 5 to 15 minutes a day to dedicate to this practice, especially when you think about how much time is spent on social media or things that aren't really critical to your day. You will find that the more you practise taking time out the easier your day will flow, and the energy you draw into your life will also be one of peace and flow. We attract what we are or what is a vibratory match to ourselves, so if we reduce our stress and raise our vibration then no matter how little or long that practice may be, we will always draw the same energy to us.

For your 30-day cauldron ritual you will need the following:

✖ a journal or notebook

✖ a cauldron or cauldrons of your choice or a small bowl

✖ an altar or shrine

✖ incense and an incense burner or a candle small enough to sit in your cauldron (optional)

✖ a crystal, stone or freshly picked flower or leaf (optional).

The intention you are setting for your 30 days is one of peace. Each day, find 5 to 15 minutes to sit at your altar or where you will not be disturbed with your cauldron or bowl and a cup of tea or a drink – preferably not coffee if you are feeling stressed. Ideally, this will be upon waking in the morning or before bed, but it can be done at any time throughout the day.

Tree of life.

Whenever I do any form of energy or spiritual work I ground myself first. The following tree of life grounding process performed every day is enough to spark a massive shift in your life, so don't underestimate the significance of grounding and protecting your energy. I do this exercise standing, to feel as much like a tree as possible. You may have your own way of doing it, so do whatever feels comfortable for you. The tree of life exercise is an extremely valuable part of any spiritual undertaking that creates your connection to the earth and to the energies above. You should draw your energy from it, just as the tree draws its energy through its roots and leaves.

✳ Stand comfortably with your feet shoulder width apart and unlock your knees. You can also do this lying down or sitting up in a seat. Find your centre and breathe out all your tension.

✳ If you are standing, rock back and forth on your feet a little to find a good position so that your balance becomes distributed evenly over your feet, and make sure you unlock your knees. Let them bend a little. You will feel any areas of tension that you need to let go of.

✳ Close your eyes and take a few deep breaths to relax and focus. Picture roots growing out of your feet and tailbone and into the earth. Send the roots down through the earth, seeing them pushing through all the layers of the earth.

✳ Picture a big white ball of energy in the centre of the earth and connect your roots to the ball of light. Picture the light from this ball moving up through your roots like a tree drawing up water and nutrients from the soil. Draw this light up through the soles of your feet and tailbone. Draw the light up through your body to your heart. It may be easier to draw the energy up on every in-breath to create a good rhythm.

✳ See the light go down to your fingertips and back to your heart. See the light go up through the centre of your head. See it extending out through branches sprouting from your head, shoulders and arms. Lift your arms to also draw the power up and to feel and become the tree. Send the energy out through the ends of the branches and out through the leaves into the sky. Watch it extend up through the layers of the atmosphere into space and reach up to touch the sun or moon (depending on the time of day), or perhaps a star.

✿ Feel the sun-, moon- or starlight on your face as you draw down its white light through your head, and trace the way back that the earth light came through you: down through your head, to your heart, to your fingertips and back to your heart, down through your body, out through your feet and through the roots. Connect with the ball of white light in the centre of the earth.

Now that you have connected like the tree of life it is important to shield yourself, which will help deflect any negative energies and will also contain the energy you now have flowing through you. Picture a big white or gold bubble in front of you that you step into, or maybe a shield that pops up all around you. Go with whatever feels right for you. Fill your shield full of white light and know you are protected. Now you can proceed with your exercise/ritual.

Once you have completed your grounding exercise, call in your spirit guides or helpers to be with you. Light a candle or incense or place a flower, leaf or crystal in your cauldron if that is where you are, or place your tea or drink in your mug.

Be in the moment and say out loud or to yourself: 'I am peace.' Calm your breathing down and feel any tension leave your body. Notice the air on your skin, listen to the sounds around you and let your mind empty itself of thoughts. If it helps you to relax, keep saying to yourself 'I am peace' or 'Body, relax.' Feel what it is like to just stop, as presence is key. When you are done, blow out the candle or incense or drink the tea. Thank spirit for joining you and then flow into your day.

You will be surprised by how much this small yet powerful ritual can be. You can do it literally anywhere, and if you don't have a vessel then be your own vessel and fill yourself up with the feeling of peace. The more you take time out to practise, the more results you will get and you will then have a steady practice of being present each and every day. This exercise will serve you well in making time for your daily spiritual practices and you will find over time that by being present, the answers to your questions will flow to you more easily and you will feel at peace. This in turn will draw more peace to you and everything will start to flow. This is the state you must aim for every day, as this is where you make grounded decisions and your entire body, mind and soul will thank you for it.

WORKING WITH PLANT AND CRYSTAL SPIRITS

As you place each herb into your cauldron, ask the plant spirit to work with you for the purpose of helping you with your intention. Always remember that you are working in co-creation with these energies, that you are not using them to get what you want. You might like to say something such as 'Every time I drink this tea, please be with me and share your knowledge so that I may learn to help and heal myself and others for their highest good.' It is important to be in the present moment, and even if you can't feel the connection to the plant spirit at this time your intent is still key. Be present, be respectful and believe in what you are doing.

Once the items you have chosen are all in your cauldron you might like to say something such as: 'Thank you, plant spirits, for joining together to aid me with my intention. I thank you and offer you my gratitude and love.' Learn to realise what it is you are truly seeking and tailor your rituals to obtain it. Life changes when we do the inner work, and this is where it starts.

CHAPTER 4

Plant Magick

Let's recap before we start. When you decide to create a ritual or ceremony for manifestation work you are not creating something that will change another person or manipulate anything. What you *are* doing is changing your internal vibration to attract what you want, which may mean you need to face situations you finally have to deal with or move on from, changing your behaviours or adding to your skill set. Whatever you encounter, realise that you have created it and it is here to teach you in order for you to achieve your goals. This is what manifestation is. In order for you to achieve what you are looking for, you must do the work and sometimes it can be incredibly hard, but the rewards await you on the other side of fear.

BREWS

Drinking teas is a beautiful way to connect with plant spirits every day. How often do you guzzle a super-sized cup of tea without really stopping to savour and smell it and feel its warmth as it travels down to your stomach? Drinking tea is my daily ritual: I not only have a myriad of teacups and teapots but also a pantry full of different teas and herbs to brew. The cauldron teacup is an absolute favourite of mine, and when I place my tea and herbs in it I connect with them and take some time out of my day to sit and enjoy the connection.

Did you know that tea has always been a revered drink in China? It was discovered by Shennong (the Divine Farmer), who brought agriculture and Chinese herbal medicine to the people. Chinese mythology tells of how a single tea leaf fell from a tree into his boiling cauldron while he was meditating, and because of his sensitivity to plant energy he instantly knew that this leaf was a special medicine. He called it the 'empress of all medicinal herbs'.

The Chinese boiled their tea in cauldrons before the process of tea manufacturing was discovered, which allowed the tea to express itself more wholly. They have a special tea ceremony in which tea is boiled for hours in a cauldron over charcoal, a process that allows for the tea to release its deepest flavours. This is the most traditional way to drink tea. I have to admit this is one of my favourite ways to drink tea. The entire ceremony is a beautiful ritual that respects the tea tree and the environment the tea is prepared in and gives the plant spirit their full attention by being in the present and doing everything with purpose.

You might have also heard about tea-leaf reading, which is known as tasseography. Loose-leaf tea is used for this ritual, and when the tea has been mostly drunk the remaining tea leaves are swirled around in the cup so the reader can use them for divination. This is a fantastic way to connect with your plant allies and guides. You don't need a special cup to do it, but there are lovely cups with symbols on the inside especially for tasseography.

Fortune teller tea cup.

All of the following recipes call for loose tea, which is not only better for the environment with no packaging but you can offer it back to your garden or compost afterwards to honour the plant. The ritual of making a tea from loose leaves and brewing them in a teapot or infuser helps to shift you into the present moment. Treat it as a self-care ritual by taking a break from what you are doing to give back to yourself.

You can use a cauldron to blend your tea first then put it straight into your teapot, tea infuser or glass jar for later use, or alternatively you might have a cauldron you use to brew the tea up in to make it an even longer ritual.

Knowing how special the tea plant is, you might like to incorporate it into many of your tea recipes or use it completely on its own. Remember that you don't need a cupboard full of herbs: you can start off with one single herb, and tea is an easy one to acquire and certainly can teach you a lifetime of lessons.

Recipe: FORTUNE TELLER TEA

This is a tea to drink before performing visionary or divination work. You can make a single cup of tea or a big batch and store it in a glass jar for later use. If you intend on storing it for later, ensure you use dried mugwort and yarrow. If you are using it for tasseography, the pieces of yarrow and mugwort need to be chopped as small as the tea leaves, as this will make it easier to read. The black tea makes up the bulk of the tea and the mugwort and yarrow will be smaller, equal quantities. I recommend 1 teaspoon of black tea per cup of tea, so for that you will need ⅓ teaspoon of mugwort and ⅓ teaspoon of yarrow.

INGREDIENTS

- ✖ 3 parts small- to medium-sized black tea leaves
- ✖ 1 part mugwort
- ✖ 1 part yarrow

DIRECTIONS

1. Mix all three herbs in a food-safe cauldron or bowl of choice.

2. Place a teaspoon of the mix into a cauldron cup, a teapot or infuser and place boiling water into the vessel. If you have a cauldron that can use a heat source, light the flame underneath it and place already boiled water in it and let the heat keep the water hot.

3. Let steep for around 5 minutes or until you reach your desired strength. This will give you time to sit longer with your herbal mixture while it steams. Smell the aroma and really take it all in. As you drink the tea, it is a good practice to thank the plant spirits and welcome them in.

If you decide to store the mixture for later you might like to add a beautiful wax seal or something such as a dried sprig of yarrow or mugwort that will make it look and feel special. Keep the mix in a place that is clean and clear of rubbish such as on your altar or in a cupboard, and always treat it with respect.

Note: yarrow increases psychic abilities and is good for protection, and mugwort is good for visionary work. However, please know you should exercise caution when ingesting mugwort as it can stimulate the uterus and menstruation, therefore avoid drinking it during pregnancy. An alternative could be bay leaf, dandelion or eyebright.

There are many herbs you might like to put together to make a beautiful brew, but it is important to ensure they are edible. Refer to Appendix I for the various uses and edibility of the herbs mentioned below. To get started I always recommend trying one herb at a time, then once you know what a few taste like you can try blending them. You could start with a base of white, green or black tea and add any of the following:

* apple, orange or lemon slices
* aniseed
* bay leaves
* bougainvillea flowers
* cacao, calendula petals, catnip leaves, chamomile flowers or cinnamon
* dandelion root
* fennel seeds
* ginger slices
* honey
* lemongrass, lemon verbena or licorice
* mint, mullein, mushrooms or mugwort
* nettle or nutmeg
* passionflower, pine needles or plantain
* rose petals, rose buds, rosehip or rosemary
* sage, self-heal, star anise or strawberry
* thyme
* valerian or vanilla.

Following are some recipes you might like to try.

Recipe: Cerridwen's brew of inspiration

We may never know what herbs Cerridwen placed in her cauldron; however, the ones that have been implied include vervain, yellow flowers of cowslip, fluxwort, hedgeberry, mistletoe berries (sacred to the Druids and said to be hallucinogenic) and foam from the ocean. It was said that Cerridwen collected the herbs at the correct times according to the stars and moon cycles.

Knowing that Cerridwen is associated with the moon, you could make up your own brew based on herbs ruled by the moon and ones for divination purposes. When you think of inspiration, knowledge and creativity what herbs would you pick? Just as you can't drink from an empty cup you can't put more into a full cup, so when you wish to acquire inspiration or find creativity do you have the space to take it on or are you full to the brim? What do you need to let go of to make room for fresh energy to find its way in?

The general rule for any brew is 1 teaspoon of herb or herbs to 1 cup of water, and below are some ideas to get you started. Pick one or a few and learn about them well:

- bay leaves for manifestation, purification and to heighten intuition
- bougainvillea for strength, protection, passion, peace and spiritual connection
- dandelion, which is ruled by the sun and moon and is good for cleansing, joy, messages and divination
- cacao, which is a heart-opening medicine
- hazelnut for wisdom
- honey for binding
- mugwort, which is ruled by the moon, for divination
- nutmeg to reveal truth and increase psychic abilities and for spiritual connection
- plantain for internal healing and drawing out
- reishi mushroom, the spirit herb, as a powder or tincture to bridge heaven and earth
- thyme for manifestation, purification and magick
- vervain to remove obstacles and bring love
- yarrow to increase psychic abilities and for protection and strength.

Recipe: dandelion joy latte

Dandelion coffee is brewed just like normal coffee, depending on which one you have. A coffee plunger is good for this or you can brew it up in your cauldron, using 1 teaspoon per cup of water.

INGREDIENTS

- ✖ 1 tsp dandelion root coffee powder per cup
- ✖ milk of your choice
- ✖ honey or maple syrup, optional

DIRECTIONS

1. Steep the root coffee and water for about 15 minutes, then add the milk and steep until the milk is warm. You can use a milk frother to heat and froth the milk.

2. Add honey if you need it to reduce the bitterness.

3. A sprinkle of nutmeg on top makes a lovely touch.

Recipe: Dagda's Cauldron of Fulfilment

INGREDIENTS

- ✖ 1 tsp cacao powder
- ✖ ½ tsp turkey tail mushroom powder
- ✖ ½ tsp rose petal powder
- ✖ milk of your choice
- ✖ honey or maple syrup, optional

DIRECTIONS

1. Heat the cacao, turkey tail and rose petal powder with the milk in a cauldron or vessel.

2. When heated to the desired temperature you might like to use a frother to froth the milk.

3. Add honey or maple syrup for sweetness if desired.

Recipe: sweet dreams brew

This is a great tea to do up in a batch and keep in a beautiful amber glass apothecary or decorated jar. This recipe uses equal ratios of each herb and you need 1 teaspoon of completely mixed tea for the recipe, so if you are making one cup use ¼ teaspoon of each ingredient.

INGREDIENTS

- ✖ 1 part passionflower
- ✖ 1 part chamomile
- ✖ 1 part rose buds
- ✖ 1 part linden flowers, optional

DIRECTIONS

1. Place the herbs in a cauldron and pour boiled water over the top.

2. Allow the mixture to steep for around 10 minutes, then drink it 30 minutes to an hour before going to bed.

Recipe: calm spirit brew

Reishi mushroom is known as the spirit herb because it is said to bridge heaven and earth and calms your spirit, making it a wonderful aid for meditation and divination.

INGREDIENTS

- 1 tsp black tea per cup (try using loose leaf tea that you can put in a mesh tea ball or teapot to steep)
- ¼ tsp reishi mushroom powder per cup (you can also buy reishi tinctures instead of powder)
- milk, optional
- honey or maple syrup, optional

DIRECTIONS

1. Brew the black tea as you normally would in a cauldron or teapot. Don't make it too strong, as it does contain some caffeine.
2. Strain and pour into a cup, then add the reishi powder to the tea and let sit for another 5 to 10 minutes.
3. Add milk and honey or maple syrup if required. Drink half an hour before ritual or meditation work and be present with the tea.

Recipe: manifestation brew

INGREDIENTS

- ✖ 1–2 bay leaves per cup of water
- ✖ cinnamon stick, optional

DIRECTIONS

1. Place the bay leaves in a cup, cauldron or teapot. As you put the bay leaves in, say what you wish to manifest. Be with the spirit of the bay leaf and enjoy the feeling of having already manifested what you want.

2. Add boiling water to the cup and steep for around 10 minutes. I like to envision the steam from the tea floating off into the ether to do its magick.

3. Many people like to add cinnamon, which has special qualities and can be placed in the vessel with the bay leaf to steep.

You may think these tea recipes are very simple but you don't need a whole lot of ingredients, and sometimes simple is best because then you are not working with lots of different energies at once.

HERBAL SIMMERS

Herbal simmer.

Do you love the smell of walking into a home that is cooking something yummy? Herbal simmers have this effect and can be used to make the air smell fresh and fragrant. Not only does it smell wonderful, but it helps release compounds of the ingredients into the air along with their spiritual and energetic properties.

A herbal simmer is much like a tea but usually something you don't drink, although you can depending on what you put in it. Fruits, spices, fragrant herbs and flowers are perfect for this and they look beautiful simmering away. Simmers can be made in most cauldrons but I would avoid cast iron if you are using any citrus fruit and don't leave the water in the cauldron after you have finished as cast iron rusts over time. Essential oil burners make a good choice, especially for small batches, and you can obviously add essential oils to the water. These can also be made on the stove in a saucepan and are known as stove potpourri.

Common fragrant herbs, spices and fruits you might like to try include:

- apple slices and skins, aniseed
- bay leaves and wild bergamot, also known as bee balm
- cacao, catnip, chamomile, cinnamon, clove, cranberries
- eucalyptus, fennel, ginger, honey and juniper
- lavender, lemongrass, lemon slices and peel, lemon verbena, licorice, lime slices and peel
- marjoram, mint, nutmeg
- orange slices and peel, oregano
- palo santo, pine needles and cones, plums
- raspberries, roses, rosehips, rosemary
- sage, star anise, strawberries
- thyme, vanilla, white sage.

I have omitted resins as they are usually heated on an incense warmer and are not placed in water (see Chapter 6 for more information about incense). You might also like to use moon water – water that has been left out overnight under moonlight – essences dropped into the water or the left-over fluid from making an essence as the water base.

DIRECTIONS

1. I like to place the ingredients into the cauldron first, then fill the rest up with boiled water. If you do it the other way around you run the risk of it overflowing. The amount of ingredients you put in depends entirely on what you have selected, and over time you will get to understand which ones you need more or less of. In saying that, even if you can't smell its aroma understand that the plant spirit will essentially be in the air all around you from the steam.

2. Each ingredient I place in I thank them for their presence and healing then light the candle or heat source. I allow it to heat and simmer gently so it releases all the beautiful aromas and essences into the air. The longer you leave it to simmer the better.

On the following pages are some recipes to get you started, but remember to look through the herb reference list in Appendix I to see if something resonates with you and feel free to substitute with other herbs if they are easier for you to obtain.

Recipe: love simmer

- ✖ sprinkle of rose petals or buds
- ✖ 2 apple slices or apple skin peelings
- ✖ 1–2 strawberries or raspberries
- ✖ pinch of a vanilla pod or ¼ tsp vanilla essence
- ✖ pinch of cinnamon

Recipe: meditation simmer

* ✖ small handful of lavender flowers
* ✖ few sprigs of thyme
* ✖ few drops of vanilla essence, infused oil or a pod
* ✖ ½ tsp black tea

Recipe: cleanse and clear simmer

* 4 eucalyptus leaves
* handful of pine needles or a pine cone
* 2 white sage leaves

Recipe: WINTER WARMTH SIMMER

- ✖ 2–3 orange peel pieces or slices
- ✖ 1 cinnamon twill
- ✖ 1 star anise
- ✖ pinch of nutmeg

Recipe: study blend simmer

- ✖ 2–3 lemon slices, lemon peel or a few leaves of lemon verbena
- ✖ handful of fresh or dried rosemary leaves
- ✖ peppermint leaves or 1 drop of essential oil

ESSENCES

Essences are a vibrational medicine that can be made in a cauldron. They are like a homeopathic medicine in that they are completely safe to use and work on an energetic level. Essences can be made from herbs, plants, rocks, crystals, flowers, trees and even shells: you can create an entire home apothecary of essences. I create flower essences from all of the flowers on my property and sometimes make combinations of crystal and flower essences when I feel it is appropriate.

Because essences are of a high vibration I recommend using a glass bowl or a ceramic or copper cauldron rather than a cast-iron one as they have very dense vibrations, but the essence will still work if that is all you have. You don't need anything too big, as a little goes a long way.

I highly recommend you create your essences from flowers, trees, plants or herbs you have growing near you, because medicine grows where it is needed and this will help you to better attune to your environment. If you are familiar with the Ogham (pronounced *o-wum*) tree alphabet you might have a set of essences made from each corresponding tree. A set of Celtic tree essences would be amazing to work with; alternatively, you can make a set of tree essences from the trees in your area. If you are a beach person you might like to create essences from shells you collect. The possibilities really are limitless!

Method: CREATING AN ESSENCE

EQUIPMENT/INGREDIENTS

- a small ceramic or copper cauldron or a glass bowl

- a cup of water to fill your cauldron (or more, depending on how large your item is), preferably the purest water you can get: collect some from your favourite stream or waterfall or catch the rain if you can do so without contamination; bottled and filtered water are also okay to use

- an item to create your essence with, such as a plant or crystal

- a glass jar if you don't want your item to get wet or the plant or crystal you wish to use is toxic, big enough to contain the item inside the cauldron: essentially, the vibration of the plant will be absorbed by the water so you don't need it to be in the water

- an amber bottle with a dropper lid for the final essence

- a small amount of brandy, vodka or gin if you wish to preserve the essence

DIRECTIONS

1. Create your essence ritual outside if possible, either in sunlight or moonlight if that is what energy you wish to use.

2. Remember to ground yourself and call in whatever helper spirits you wish to work with.

3. Fill the cauldron with water, leaving some room at the top.

4. Place your chosen plant matter or item on top of the water, into the water or in another vessel within the water to keep it dry.

5. Leave the cauldron brewing in sunlight for around 4 hours or overnight in moonlight. Place a light piece of fabric over the cauldron if you're worried things might fall in it, but understand that what falls in may also be medicine in itself so go with your intuition on this.

6. When the time has passed, thank the items and spirits that have worked with you and strain the water into a bottle, jar or Pyrex jug. You can use the essence straight away; it will last for approximately seven days.

7. If you wish to preserve the essence indefinitely, fill an amber bottle with a dropper lid halfway with essence and top with the chosen alcohol.

Dosage: 7 drops of essence under your tongue morning and night or when needed.

Recipe: PROTECTION ESSENCE

- ✖ yarrow, white or pink
- ✖ rowan bark, Ogham stave or Ogham symbol or leaf, optional
- ✖ holly or blackthorn, optional
- ✖ black tourmaline crystal, optional

Use this essence when you need protection or if you are feeling vulnerable. You might also use it before you start your ritual or ceremony or before leaving the house to go to a crowded space.

Recipe: cleansing essence

✖ sage or white sage

✖ rosemary

✖ palo santo

This recipe is great for making sacred palo santo go further. Use one stick in the jar or bowl within the cauldron to prevent it getting wet. Alternatively, you can infuse palo santo in vodka for a month or more and then place a few drops in your finished essence.

Use the cleansing essence before starting a ritual or ceremony or when you are feeling overwhelmed by external sources. You could put the essence into a diffuser to spread it throughout your space or include it in a herbal simmer or brew.

Recipe: oak tree essence

✖ oak Ogham stave, optional

✖ oak leaves, catkins, acorns or bark
(you can use one part or all of them)

You might like to place an Ogham symbol on the oak leaves. You can find the Ogham symbols in Appendix III. The oak tree represents strength, endurance, protection and a doorway to other worlds.

Use this essence when meditating or shamanic journeying as well as when you need strength, guidance, grounding, wisdom and endurance.

Recipe: pine tree essence

✖ pine needles, bark, resin or cones

Use pine essence when you are in need of protection and healing. The cone also helps with new beginnings and letting go.

Recipe: elder flower essence

✖ elder flowers

Elder flowers are used for strength, regeneration, endings and healing. This is a terrific essence for internal work.

Recipe: self-heal essence

✖ self-heal plant or flowers

This is an amazing essence to work on internal issues and heal from the inside. It is also an aid for growing and learning from your wounds.

MAGICKAL LOTIONS

A cauldron book wouldn't be complete without magickal lotions, right? The great thing about lotions is that you can use a brew or herbal simmer. I mean, you could go to the trouble of making a cream from scratch, which is rewarding in itself because you can use your own herbal brews and infused oils, but if you don't have the time, patience or ingredients to go down that route you can take some of the water from your brew or herbal simmer and combine it with a natural body cream you already have.

One thing to note is that the base cream you use should be as natural as possible. Base creams are simply just water and oil with an emulsifier, vitamin E and a preservative. Many herbalists still use base creams, which can be very effective for a number of reasons: they are able to correct certain skin conditions and contain a preservative, so once added they should be quite stable.

> *Note: your base cream must already have water included in it for you to be able to add liquid. If you try to put water into a cream that is just oil then the water and oil will not blend.*

METHOD: MAGICKAL LOTION

---

1. What is the intention of your lotion? You will need to think about that before you make the brew or herbal simmer, or you might just like to work more with the brew or herbal simmer by making it into a lotion.

2. Ensure any herb you use in your brew or herbal simmer is okay to use on skin. Please research what you use and make notes in your notebook about each herb and plant.

3. The amount of fluid you can place into a cream will be dependent on what cream you use and how much. The general rule is you can add in liquid about 10 to 20 per cent of the total weight of your cream, so if the jar you are using takes 100 g/3.5 oz you can normally squeeze about 10 ml/0.3 fl oz of liquid in. Add the liquid in small amounts and stir until thoroughly combined, repeating if necessary, until no more will combine, which means the cream has reached its limit.

Notes

- × You can also add a little infused oil, essential oils or even a couple of drops of an essence to your lotion if you like.

- × If you are adding a brew that is still hot or warm you need to let the cream cool down before putting on the lid, or it will sweat and very quickly create mould in your cream.

On the following pages are suggestions of ingredients you might like to try for your lotions. You don't need all of them; just pick something you have or can make. I've included some affirmations you might like to say when you rub it on your skin.

Self-healing

Self-heal plant.

- self-heal brew, herbal simmer, infused oil or essence: any or all of these can be used; the herb self-heal heals inside and out
- calendula brew, infused oil or essence; also a skin healer
- plantain brew, infused oil or essence; heals wounds and draws things out
- rose petal brew, infused oil or essence for self-love
- vervain brew or essence; a remover of obstacles
- sunflower brew or essence for strength and optimism
- elder flower brew or essence for healing and new beginnings
- essences using green or pink stones or crystals.

Affirmation: 'I heal from the inside out.'

Protection

Nettle leaf.

* nettle leaf brew, herbal simmer or infused oil; also good for itchy skin conditions such as eczema
* mullein brew, infused oil or essence
* yarrow brew, infused oil or essence
* thyme brew or essence
* star anise brew or essence
* bougainvillea brew or essence
* essences using black tourmaline, black onyx, yarrow, pine, heather, holly or rowan
* essential oils using myrrh or sandalwood.

Affirmation: 'I am grounded and protected.'

Abundance

- ✖ allspice brew
- ✖ basil brew or essence
- ✖ oregano brew or essence
- ✖ pine brew or essence
- ✖ honey
- ✖ citrine essence
- ✖ essential oils using palo santo or patchouli.

Affirmation: 'I am abundant in all areas.'

MAGICKAL POTIONS

A cauldron book also wouldn't be complete without magickal potions! Potions are sometimes called elixirs and they are normally drunk immediately after preparation or used in various other ways such as:

- an essence
- anointing water to consecrate special tools or call in the spirit of the plant
- spray mist as a room spray or body mist
- asperging, which means sprinkling water on an object or area you wish to cleanse or imbue with your intent.

When I am close to finishing with my potion I like to offer a small bit back to the earth in appreciation and to honour the spirits that have worked with me. This also allows the intent to flow through the ground and off in every direction.

LOVE POTIONS

When working with love potions you must understand that you cannot force someone against their will and you cannot ask for a specific person to love you. Why? Because the person you might think is the right person for you may not be. We need to be open to other possibilities that we can't necessarily see and may need to let go of baggage that is stopping us from being in alignment with our true partner. We may need to learn to love ourselves first before we can call in a partner. There are many reasons why we may not be drawing love to us and that is the most important thing to put our focus into. We need to focus on shifting the blocks around finding love.

Finding items that give you a sense of love is critical for your love potion. I associate red wine and candlelight with love, as well as rose quartz, rose petals and even my cat, so how do I incorporate all this into a love potion? I start by adding the base liquid red wine to my cauldron. I then add organic rose petals, vervain and a piece of rose quartz crystal and I light a candle. I radiate the feeling of love, starting by picturing my cat. I know: bear with me here! Whenever I think of my cat it makes me smile and I feel my heart open; I love her unconditionally, and she loves me back. This emotion of love makes me a vibrational match to love and being loved is the feeling you must feel in the present moment.

Recipe: vervain and rose wine potion

Use this potion in ritual when you want to bring in love.

INGREDIENTS

- around 50 ml/1.7 fl oz red wine
- sprinkle of organic rose petals with no pesticides
- sprinkle of vervain

DIRECTIONS

1. Create your ritual space, perform the tree of life grounding exercise (see Chapter 3) and call in your helper spirits. Call upon the plant spirits of rose and vervain to be with you and infuse into your wine for your healing and guidance. Ask for them to share their wisdom, and if you are using it for love state that you wish to find love in whatever way that looks like for your highest good. Really be in the moment.

2. Add the ingredients to a heatproof cauldron and heat very gently while stirring. Don't let it boil; but just let it come to a good heat. As you stir the mixture try to feel the plant spirits with you and infusing into your wine.

3. Take off the heat and strain. When cooled slightly, take a sip. When you drink the preparation be present and savour the smell, taste and feel. Respect the process. Say to yourself or out loud: 'I attract love, I *am* love.'

Record everything in your notebook, thank the plant spirits for their help and actually allow the plant spirits to help you. It took around three months for love to find me, with different experiences happening over that time until I had my 'aha' moment. Once that occurred my whole life began to change because I had a different perception of myself, so my outer world had to shift to match my inner one.

Recipe: abundance potion

Abundance potions are very much like love potions: we must become a vibrational match to what we wish to attract. We may have abundance all around us – which we all do – but are we open to receiving? If not, that may be the issue an abundance potion will bring to the surface for you to work on, or perhaps it will bring up whether you feel worthy of what you want. It is only when we work on the core issue of our lack of abundance that we will get closer to our goals. It may be hard to look at and uncomfortable, but that is the gift the plant spirits offer us. They know the way, and this is how they show us. We only acquire blocks in order to learn from them, then once we learn the lesson the energy shifts and we change our vibration and become one with what we wish to manifest.

Perhaps you would like to change the name of this abundance potion to 'I am open to receiving potion', or you could make this your affirmation as you drink it.

INGREDIENTS

✖ pinch of allspice
✖ 1 small cup red wine
✖ 1–2 orange slices or juice
✖ ½ tsp honey
✖ 1–2 drops of citrine crystal essence

DIRECTIONS

Follow the same directions as for the vervain and rose wine potion.

Recipe: ᵹʀᴀᴄɪᴄᴜᴅᴇ ᴘoᴄɪoɴ

Giving our gratitude and sitting in the feeling of gratitude raises our vibration to an extremely high level. When we sit in this feeling and are grateful for what we have in our lives we draw more things to be grateful for into it, which is why gratitude diaries are so great. When we start to recognise the positive in our lives we take our focus off the negative in that instant, which shifts our vibration to attracting positivity instead of negativity.

I know that sometimes it's hard to see the positives in our lives, which is what makes a gratitude potion so perfect: not only will it help you to remember to be grateful, it will help you see how to be grateful and help raise your vibration to draw in more gratitude. This simple act can be life changing, so don't underestimate the power of positivity. If you don't have some or all of the ingredients look for a substitute or be guided by your intuition about what else you could include.

EQUIPMENT/INGREDIENTS

- a cauldron with a heat source
- ¼ tsp reishi powder or tincture (the spirit herb)
- 1 tsp cacao (heart opener)
- 1 tsp cacao butter, optional
- pinch of cinnamon (increases psychic ability)
- pinch of nutmeg (increases psychic and spiritual connections)
- ½ tsp honey, optional
- 3 drops of sunflower oil or essence (optimism)
- 3 drops of quartz or amethyst essence
- milk of your choice
- boiled water
- you could also burn some incense with frankincense or sandalwood while you are making or using your potion for increased benefits

DIRECTIONS

1. Place the first six ingredients with intent into the cauldron.

2. Light the heat source and add the boiled water to keep the potion simmering. You can also add the milk now to heat it up.

3. Stir the mixture thoroughly and call on the spirit of each of the plants. Feel your gratitude pouring into your potion.

4. Allow the mixture to brew for about 10 minutes, then add milk if it hasn't already been added.

5. Add the essences now if you are using them.

6. As you drink the potion, sit in a feeling of gratitude. Record in your journal what you are grateful for today: you could be grateful for the sun or wind on your face. It doesn't have to be big things, as sometimes the best things in life are the small ones.

7. Give some of your potion back to the earth.

Recipe: MOON POTION

The Celts followed the lunar calendar, and we are all aware of the amazing qualities of the moon and its cycles. This is a beautiful potion for utilising the moon's energies and a full moon is perfect, as during that cycle the moon is in its best energetic position.

EQUIPMENT/INGREDIENTS

- a cauldron to place outside under the moon (don't use cast iron as the lemon will interact with it)
  - ✖ 1 tsp mugwort
  - ✖ squeeze of lemon juice, seeds or rind
  - ✖ 3 drops of moonstone or quartz crystal or essence
  - ✖ 3 drops of willow tree essence (you can create your own using the Ogham symbol for willow if you don't have the physical plant; see Appendix III)
  - ✖ 1 cup water, white wine or coconut water
  - ✖ myrrh incense to burn during the ritual, optional; it can also be used to smoke the inside of your cauldron, which cleanses it and adds its qualities to your potion

DIRECTIONS

1. A full moon is perfect for this potion as the moon is at its best energetic position although any phase is still fine, depending on your intent.

2. You might like to take your fluid out with you in a jug so you can pour it into your cauldron under the moonlight with your intent.

3. Place the moonstone crystal or quartz in the bottom of your cauldron.

4. Add the mugwort, lemon and essence.

5. Pour in the chosen liquid and stir, making sure you are fully present and calling the moon into your potion. Be present with

this mix for as long as you feel necessary; you can even leave it out for a few hours if you choose.

6. Strain the mixture.

7. Depending on what you used you may or may not like the taste of your potion, but you can now:

* drink some

* create an essence from it by filling an amber drop bottle halfway and then topping up with alcohol such as brandy

* store the potion in a bottle for a couple of days and use it to make offerings to the earth

* use it as a spray for asperging sacred tools or calling in moon energy.

Recipe: ANCESTORS' POTION

This is a beautiful creation for helping you connect with your ancestors: all those who have gone before us, not just our family lineage. The collective knowledge the ancestors hold is wisdom we can tap into at any time. Call upon the ancestors when you are working with this potion and allow them to help you with the answers you seek.

EQUIPMENT/INGREDIENTS

- a cauldron that you can boil water in for around 15 minutes
  - ✖ 1 tsp or 1 teabag black tea (brings people together)
  - ✖ pinch of hazelnut (strong connection with wisdom)

✻ pinch of nutmeg (increases spiritual connection)

✻ pinch of oak leaf (access to the other realms)

✻ pinch of reishi (the spirit herb)

✻ 1 cup of water

✻ essences using grounding stones or Preseli bluestone (my favourite; see Appendix II)

DIRECTIONS

1. Depending on the capability of your cauldron, you can either place boiled water into it or heat the water from scratch in it.

2. Place the tea in the water.

3. Grind up the hazelnut, nutmeg, oak leaf and reishi as small as you can and place them in the water.

4. Boil for 15 minutes then strain.

5. Once cool, add any essences you like to the mix.

6. For this potion I like to drop a small amount into a big glass of water to sip during ritual. Alternatively, you might like to use it as scrying water or a mist to spray around your ritual space, or add it to your bath.

7. Just like the three drops from Cerridwen's cauldron were powerful enough to gift all the wisdom of the world, a little goes a long way. Note that all of the ingredients apart from the essence are related to trees: the wisdom keepers and the ones that are firmly grounded in the earth where our ancestors lie.

Recipe: STRENGTH POTION

This potion is excellent for those times when you feel vulnerable or run down or need inner strength to face something.

EQUIPMENT/INGREDIENTS

- a cauldron to take outside that will hold water
- a sunny day
- any of the following: bougainvillea bracts (the pink, purple or bright red parts that look like flowers), borage, dandelion flowers, elder flowers, oak leaves, saffron, self-heal, thyme or any herb or plant of your choice from Appendix I that is edible
- water
- sunflower, waratah or oak essence
- crystal essences made from dark-coloured or red stones for grounding and your base chakra such as black tourmaline, red jasper, ruby

DIRECTIONS

1. Place each dry ingredient you have chosen into your cauldron with intent and purpose.

2. Fill the cauldron with water.

3. Add the essences. If the cauldron has a lid, feel free to put it on.

4. Leave the mixture to sit for 1 hour in the full sun then strain.

5. Enjoy as a drink, an offering to the earth to release your intention, a spray mist or make into an essence.

Recipe: boundaries potion

Setting boundaries for yourself is a healthy practice. It doesn't mean putting up a wall that doesn't allow anything in; rather, it means you define what you will and will not allow to enter your space. It also means you need to find your inner strength in order to set and keep the boundaries, and a boundaries potion will help to bring it all together. Because there are so many different herbs you could pick

I've listed only a few suggestions. Make sure whatever you put in is ingestible, then use it as a spray mist or anointing water. When you use spray mists bear in mind that you can inhale them, which is classed as being ingested. Also check that the herbs are safe for use around animals.

Pick whichever herbs you can get your hands on from the list below or use ones that you know would be a good substitute: ½ teaspoon of each herb you have. The vodka is only necessary if you intend to store the potion; otherwise, use it within two days as the high herb content will make it go off.

EQUIPMENT/INGREDIENTS

- cauldron
- basil (banishing)
- garlic (banishing, healing, protection)
- mullein (standing tall, strength, grounding, courage, protection)
- nettle (threshold guardian, protection, banishing)
- star anise (cord cutting, protection)
- tarragon (strength and independence after abuse, banishing, confidence)
- thyme (protection, courage, strength)
- yarrow (boundaries, protection)
- yellow dock (cord cutting, clearing blockages, understanding)
- 3 drops of blackthorn essence (you can create your own using the Ogham symbol for blackthorn if you don't have the physical plant; see Appendix III)
- 3 drops of St John's wort essence (finding your centre)

✖ 3 drops of sunflower essence (inner
strength, joy, optimism)

✖ 3 drops of either black onyx or obsidian crystal essence

✖ ½ cup vodka (if you intend to keep it;
alternatively, use within two days as the
high herb content will make it go off)

✖ ½ cup water (1 cup if not using the vodka)

DIRECTIONS

1. Place the water or water and vodka mix into the cauldron.

2. Chop the herbs into small pieces, although the star anise can be left whole.

3. Place the herbs in the cauldron and stir in your chosen intention.

4. Allow the mixture sit for 24 hours then strain.

5. Add the essences and pour into a spray bottle.

Recipe: SERENITY POTION

Who doesn't need a serenity potion from time to time? I mean, you could just drink your herb-preserving vodka, but that isn't the best solution. This potion will help you find your inner calm, centre and quiet space so you can get through the toughest of times, or you could simply use it regularly to give yourself some self-care just because you can.

EQUIPMENT/INGREDIENTS

- cauldron that can tolerate boiled water and with a lid
- ½ tsp California poppy (relaxation, regeneration, peace)
- ½ tsp chamomile (rest, peace)
- ½ tsp fennel seeds (calming)
- ½ tsp passionflower (relaxation)
- 1 cup boiled water
- 3 drops of yarrow essence (balance, peace, positivity)
- 3 drops of willow essence (support, helps with emotions)
- 3 drops of scolecite essence (alternatives are amethyst, black tourmaline or rose quartz)

DIRECTIONS

1. Place the herbs in the cauldron while stating your intention.
2. Pour the boiled water over them and put on a lid.
3. After 15 minutes of steeping, strain the water into a cauldron cup or mug.
4. Once the mixture has cooled a little, add the essences.
5. You can discard the herbs back to the earth, placing your intention as you bury them, or put them on a compost heap that you ask if it can take your worries or stress from you and transform them. Alternatively, you can add the herbs to your bath water, although they must be used straight away.
6. This is a potion you can drink, and the physical actions will be relaxing and calming. Then make some time for you.

Chapter 5

Anointing oils, salves and melts

Infused oils and salves are very easy to make when you get the hang of it: you'll start to acquire a nice little apothecary of various herbs that have myriad uses. I suggest you start with just one herb and build from there, because it can get a bit overwhelming.

Working with plants and your cauldron brings a lot of satisfaction, because you truly are creating a magickal finished product. You can use infused oils and salves for many things and anointing objects and yourself is just one. 'Anointing' means to rub or smear an oil onto something as part of a ceremony. You might like to anoint the outside of a candle, a bowl or item you're working with, or you can anoint yourself by rubbing the oil or salve onto skin areas such as your temples or the insides of your wrists. The point of anointing is to be present and call in the specific energy you wish to work with.

Other ways in which you might want to use your oil include:

* Scrying by placing a few drops in a cauldron full of water.
* Placing a few drops in your bath to call in the plant spirit for a particular intention.
* Edible oils and herbs that are safe to ingest can be used in magickal cooking creations and on salads; for example, rosemary-infused olive oil.
* If it's safe to do so you can place a small percentage of the oil into cream to be used on your skin as a special-intent cream. If you are an advanced cream maker you could use the infused oil as your oil phase in a cream.

For this section you do need to ensure you use a cauldron that can safely be heated for the salves or oils. Double boilers are now used to make oils and salves, but nearly everything used to be made in cauldrons so I see it as optional to use either a cauldron as it is, or create a double boiler for it. For making a small jar of salve you can even use an oil burner that is used for heating essential oils.

To create a double boiler, place a trivet, vegetable steamer or similar in the cauldron to keep the second vessel from touching the bottom where it will be the hottest. This is very important when heating oils as they can catch fire if they get too hot, but if you have a very low flame, are completely present with the oil and perform the process quickly you can do without it. If you are making large quantities I suggest you try a double boiler to start with, as it is the safest and is easy to clean up afterwards.

Double boiler.

Notes on preserving oils and salves: if you intend to keep your salve or oil for a long time, it is recommended you add vitamin E, which is an antioxidant, to prevent the oil from oxidising and going rancid. However, if you only make small batches and use them quickly then vitamin E is not needed and the oil or salve can sometimes last up to one year if stored away from sunlight and heat. Whatever the amount of oil or salve you have you only need 1 per cent of it to be vitamin E, so for 100 g/3.5 oz of oil you need 1 g/0.03 oz of vitamin E.

If you choose to add vitamin E please be aware that it is not heat stable, so it should be added to the oil when it is starting to cool. Do not heat it up with the other ingredients and do not ingest it.

Below are some suggestions for herbs that make great anointing oils or salves:

* Bay leaf, the manifestation herb that represents victory, peace, clairvoyance, purification, heightens intuition, wards off negative energy and eases anxiety and stress.
* Calendula, a flower of warmth and movement that not only helps with moving stagnant energy within us, but also works on the sacral chakra and externally for skin issues. Use the whole flower, not just the petals.
* Dandelion for joy, optimism, pain and sore muscles. Pick the yellow flowers when they open and let them wilt for a day before placing them in the oil.
* Lavender is great for meditation, relaxation, anxiety, burns and wounds.
* Mugwort is one of those herbs that should be a staple item in any magickal cupboard: it has so many uses and can be readily found. It is mainly used for visionary work and protection, but you can also rub some of this salve on the soles of your feet before going to bed to encourage dreams and restful sleep.
* Palo santo for cleansing, grounding, sacredness and transformation. Only use it if it is from a sustainable and reputable source. Palo santo needs to be ground down to very fine dust to be infused in the oil; I infuse it for an entire lunar month.
* Plantain for internal healing on a metaphysical level and drawing out what does not serve you.
* Rose, the flower of love. Different flower colours signify different types of emotions.
* Rosemary, the memory herb, helps with cleansing and protection. Remove all the leaves from the stem before placing them in the oil.
* Self-heal to give you the strength to heal inside and out and spiritual connection.
* Vervain, the herb of love and remover of obstacles.
* White sage, which is such a rewarding plant to grow. I know that I am doing my bit for its sustainability by growing it myself. White sage is for cleansing and protection and holds the wisdom of knowledge and clarity. Call on white sage when you need guidance.

ANOINTING OILS

Please note that anything that will be applied to your skin, eaten or breathed in should *always* be made in a *food-safe cauldron*, because you don't know what chemicals may be lurking in the vessel and it is better to be safe than sorry.

You will need to choose a plant you are drawn to or resonate with and check that it is safe to handle and is safe for the skin. I like to work with just one herb at a time so I fully make a connection with it and understand what its message is. When you combine herbs it can be difficult to tell what is doing what, so when you know what you are doing you can experiment with different combinations if that appeals to you.

In order to make a salve you first need a herb-infused oil. My book *Plant Spirit Medicine* goes into great detail on the many ways in which you can make these. If you don't have an appropriate oil yet that's okay, because you can make one in a cauldron using the fast-heat method. Alternatively, you can use the folk method of filling a jar halfway with the chosen herb or plant then covering it with oil and keeping it warm somewhere out of direct sunlight for a month. Once strained, the oil will keep for up to a year without an antioxidant if it is stored in a cool, dark place.

Below are instructions for both the fast-heat method and the folk method, which is the most common one.

Method 1, fast heat: **infused oil**

EQUIPMENT/INGREDIENTS

- oil of your choice such as sweet almond, olive or jojoba
- herb/s of your choice
- blender or mortar and pestle
- glass preserving jar to place your oil or salve into: not all glass jars will be able to tolerate hot liquid, so ensure it is a preserving or Mason jar
- scales: preferably to two decimal places although one decimal place is fine
- cauldron with a heat source or a double boiler
- glass beaker, optional
- vegetable steamer or stand, optional

DIRECTIONS

The amount of oil you use will depend on the size of the cauldron or vessel and the amount of herb or plant you have. It is important that you cut down plant material to small-sized pieces to allow for the oil to penetrate it. There are no specific measurements for the oil apart from ensuring that all herbs and plants are covered by it.

1. If you are using a double boiler, put the vegetable stand inside the cauldron then pour in boiled water.

2. Place the herbs and oil into the glass jar or beaker or straight into the cauldron if you are not using a double boiler and gently heat it. Don't let the oil bubble, as this will be too hot.

3. Set your intention and call on the plant spirit to be with you and imbue your oil.

4. Heat the oil until you can see it change colour: it usually goes a shade of green depending on the plant material. If you can't notice a change in colour just heat it for around 15 minutes, all the while ensuring it does not bubble.

5. Strain the herb from the oil while it is still warm using a muslin cloth, tea towel or pillow case and place the oil in the jar. Once it has completely cooled, put the lid on the jar.

6. Thank the plant spirit for being with you.

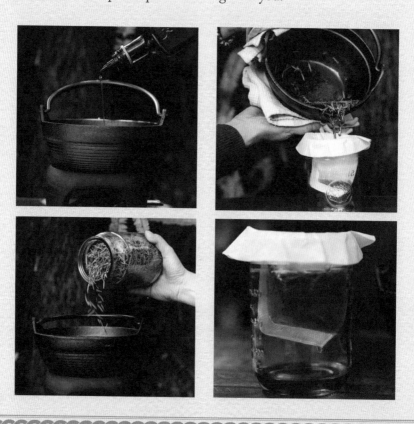

Method 2, folk method: iꜰᴜsed oil

EQUIPMENT/INGREDIENTS

- blender or mortar and pestle
- jar to place your oil in
- oil of your choice such as sweet almond, olive, jojoba
- herb/s of your choice; if the herb has a lot of water content you might like to let it wilt overnight before working with it

DIRECTIONS

1. Grind down the plant matter as much as possible with the blender and place it in the jar. Fill to only around halfway as some plants can swell once the oil is added so they need the extra room.

2. Pour the oil over the herb making sure it is covered completely, because any herb that sticks above the oil has the potential to go mouldy.

3. Cover the jar and place it somewhere warm for a minimum of two weeks and up to a month. I like to store it for a month as then it covers an entire moon phase.

4. Once it has sat for the required time, strain the herb from the oil and place the oil into a clean jar, with or without vitamin E, and ensure you label it with the name of the oil and when you created it.

SALVES

Lavender salve.

One of my favourite items is anointing salves, which are fun and easy to make and most of all give you a product at the end that is portable and can be used anywhere. Lavender salves are amazing for healing: I take one everywhere I go just in case and they are great to take camping for mosquito bites, burns and scrapes.

Recipe: basic salve

Below are the measurements to fill one small lip-balm container of 15 g/0.5 oz, but if you wish to learn how to make larger quantities I suggest you refer to my book *Plant Spirit Medicine*, in which I give you the calculations for making the exact quantities you need for any given jar.

Oil burner.

EQUIPMENT/INGREDIENTS

- cauldron with heat source (you can use a regular oil burner for making a small jar of salve)
- a second vessel and trivet for inside the cauldron as per making the anointing oils if you are using the double boiler method
- a teaspoon or something to stir the salve as the wax is melting
- paper towels
- tea towel or oven mitt
- small lip balm–sized jar or small container (aluminium or glass is best)

> ✖ 12.45 g/0.45 oz infused plant oil of your choice
> ✖ 2.40 g/0.08 oz beeswax or candelilla wax
> ✖ 0.15 g/0.005 oz vitamin E, optional

The total weight is 15 g/0.53 oz.

DIRECTIONS

1. Set your intention and call on the plant spirit to be with you and present in your salve.

2. If you are using a double boiler, place the trivet in the bottom, pour boiled water into the cauldron then add the second vessel with the oil and wax inside.

3. If you are using just a cauldron, put the oil and wax in now.

4. Heat the oil and wax and stir with the teaspoon until the wax completely melts.

5. As soon as the wax is melted, remove the hot vessel with the tea towel and pour it into the jar.

6. If you are using vitamin E, let the mix cool slightly before adding it and stir well before pouring into the container.

7. Let the mixture cool before putting on the lid or it will sweat.

8. Thank the plant spirit for being with you.

I sometimes like to place a small tumbled crystal in the bottom of the container I pour my salve into. Any quartz is good for this, as they can withstand heat and won't interfere with the salve in any way. I ask the crystal to help me connect more wholly with the plant spirit when I use the salve. Once the salve is finished you will have your crystal back again and can refill your container.

Use these crystals for specific intentions:

✖ clear or white quartz for amplification, channelling, universal truth and higher consciousness
✖ rose quartz for love
✖ black tourmaline for protection and grounding.

When it comes to using the salve, call on the plant or crystal spirit to be with you. You might like to anoint your wrists or temples before meditating, journeying or divination. Really be present, and feel with all your senses for the plant spirit.

Below are some quick and easy salve recipes that you might like to get started with. If you wish to combine two or more herbal oils together this is fine; just work with your intuition and with the herbs and plants that work in a similar manner for the one intention. When using essential oils it is best to keep the percentage to 1 per cent of the mix, so if you are making a small 15 g/0.5 oz container of salve you need just 0.15 g/0.005 oz, which is around five drops.

Use the measurements and directions in the basic salve recipe to create the following salves.

Recipe: meditation and calmness salve

* ✖ lavender-infused oil
* ✖ wax of your choice
* ✖ lavender essential oil, optional
* ✖ vitamin E, optional

Use lavender salve whenever you need to find some calm, reduce anxiety, or wish to meditate. Place it on the insides of your wrist, your temples or the soles of your feet. It is also great for closed-wound burns, bites and infections that are red and raised under the skin.

Recipe: VISIONARY AND DIVINATION SALVE

- ✖ mugwort-infused oil
- ✖ wax of your choice
- ✖ vitamin E, optional

Mugwort salve is good for rubbing on the soles of your feet before going to bed for a restful sleep and prophetic dreams and before divination work.

Recipe: PROTECTION SALVE

- ✖ yarrow-infused oil
- ✖ wax of your choice
- ✖ black tourmaline tumble stone

Use this yarrow salve when you want to protect yourself from external influences or while working in groups of people. It is a great salve for when you are travelling or to use when meditating or journeying.

Recipe: cleansing and clarity salve

- ✖ white sage–infused oil
- ✖ wax of your choice
- ✖ vitamin E, optional

I reserve my white-sage salve for anointing and working in ceremony or ritual. Being such a sacred herb, I call on its wisdom and purity as it helps me see things from a higher perspective.

Recipe: love salve

- ✖ vervain-infused oil
- ✖ wax of your choice
- ✖ rose quartz tumble stone
- ✖ vitamin E, optional

This is a beautiful salve to use when you need to feel or find love. Finding love usually starts with how you love yourself, so this is what you may experience first.

Recipe: joy and release salve

- ✖ dandelion-infused oil from the flowers
- ✖ wax of your choice
- ✖ vitamin E, optional

Use the joy and release salve when you need to shift anger or fear to find joy and be uplifted. It is also good for aches and pains.

Recipe: deep-healing salve

- ✖ plantain-infused oil from the leaves
- ✖ wax of your choice
- ✖ vitamin E, optional

Use this salve on skin wounds and when you need to draw out something deep from within to heal on a metaphysical level. It can also be used to draw out foreign items from under your skin and heal wounds.

MELTS

Wax melt.

Wax melts are a lovely creation for your cauldron, because not only can you make them in it but you can then burn them in the cauldron. Designed to melt in an oil burner or electric wax melter, they smell absolutely beautiful and you can make them with so many different ingredients and for so many different intentions. I prefer to make all-natural ones and use a reusable silicone mould instead of the plastic boxes that are designed for them.

When it comes to waxes you can use beeswax or candelilla (plant) wax, and for the oil I prefer to use coconut. You can infuse the coconut oil beforehand with your chosen herb to give it more qualities, smell or colour, or you can add chopped-up parts of herbs that release their aroma from the melt when they are heated. Melts are usually made with highly scented ingredients because it is the aroma that people enjoy; however, if you're making melts for a particular intention it is the spirit of the plant and ingredients that matter so don't be put off if they don't smell. Smells can evoke emotions within us, like the smell of coffee or spices in the air, so also think of what smell would invoke a specific feeling from within.

You can get plant powders that you might like to infuse the coconut oil with beforehand as well such as indigo (blue), chlorella (green), alkanet root powder (pink), annatto (yellow/orange) and so on. They will fade over time, but they look amazing if you use them fairly quickly. These need to be heated together in a double boiler for about 10 minutes and then strained. The great thing about melts is that they are reusable, because you don't have to use them all straight away and they are environmentally friendly!

HERBS

Below are herbs you might like to use for their scents:

- allspice
- bergamot
- cacao, catnip, chamomile, cinnamon, clove
- eucalyptus

- lavender, lemon rind, lime rind
- mint
- nutmeg
- orange rind, oregano
- palo santo, pine
- rose, rosemary
- thyme
- vanilla, vetiver
- white sage.

You might use these herbs to look pretty, which will also add their qualities:

- bougainvillea bracts, borage flowers
- calendula petals, chamomile flowers, cloves, dandelion flowers
- hawthorn flowers
- lavender flowers, lemon rind, lime rind
- orange rind, pine needles
- rose petals or buds, rosemary leaves or flowers
- saffron, star anise
- thyme leaves or flowers
- vervain leaves or flowers
- yarrow flowers (any colour).

ESSENTIAL OILS

I use essential oils very sparingly so my knowledge of them is limited, but here are the most common ones that will make your home smell amazing:

- cedarwood, cinnamon, clove, cypress
- eucalyptus
- frankincense
- ginger, grapefruit
- jasmine (normally comes as 3 per cent in oil)
- lavender, lemon, lime
- orange
- palo santo, patchouli, peppermint, pine
- rosemary

- sandalwood, Scots pine, silver fir
- vanilla, vetiver
- ylang ylang.

> *Note: please do check that the oils you use are safe to be burned around your pets, as some can be toxic.*

Beautiful essential-oil combinations I like for their aroma include:

- lavender and peppermint
- vanilla and orange
- cinnamon, clove, ginger and nutmeg.

You will need to start off with a basic recipe and then add ingredients to it once it has melted. If you choose to use essential oils, ensure they are from a sustainable source. A massive amount of plant matter is needed to produce small amounts of essential oil, and many oils are made from plants that are rapidly declining in numbers and even becoming endangered. Some reputable businesses grow their own plants to turn into essential oils and other products, so do your research about where you source your oils and what type you are using.

Some oils such as palo santo must be from a sustainable supplier who produces oil only from branches that have fallen naturally and thus the tree is protected, although overharvesting can have lasting effects on the forest around it. There are many sustainable palo santo suppliers that are replanting palo santo and harvesting it in an ethical manner. Frankincense and sandalwood are two other trees you must ensure are from sustainable sources. We need to support people who are doing the right thing with sustainable practices by buying their products and not encourage suppliers using unsustainable practices. It is up to you to make a personal choice by doing your research and trusting your intuition. If it doesn't feel right there are always many other substitutes. Let spirit be your guide.

Sometimes I try to get aromas from the other ingredients I put in my products, and if I feel it needs an essential oil I will use some. Fragrances are synthetic, so if you want fragrance please use an essential oil. There are also natural fragrances on the market that are made similarly to essential oils, but they only extract or isolate the molecule that gives off the smell and not the full-plant profile that would be achieved with essential oils. I have not used these, so it might be a personal decision for you to make should you wish to try them out. Again, just do your research and trust your gut.

Method: **basic wax melt**

EQUIPMENT/INGREDIENTS

- cauldron with a heat source or a double boiler
- a mould that is able to tolerate heat
  (I use silicone chocolate moulds)
- ✖ 100 g/3.5 oz beeswax
- ✖ 50 g/1.8 oz coconut oil
- ✖ up to 3 g/0.1 oz essential oil/s of your choice
- ✖ herbs and/or crystals of your choice

DIRECTIONS

1. Place the herbs or crystals into the mould and set aside.
2. Heat the beeswax and coconut oil in the cauldron or double boiler until they have both melted.
3. Remove from the heat and allow the mixture to cool a little before adding the essential oils, as they are affected by high heat.
4. Pour the mixture into the mould and place in the freezer until set.

5. Pop the shapes out of the mould and into your cauldron or wax burner and enjoy!

You might like to try the following essential oils and combinations with the basic wax melt recipe.

Recipe: uplift wax melt

* use up to 3 g/0.1 oz of any of the following essential oils or combinations: sandalwood, orange, rose or palo santo
* herbs, flowers or crystals of your choice (amethyst or clear quartz would be good)

Recipe: meditation wax melt

* use up to 3 g/0.1 oz of any of the following essential oils or combinations: frankincense, lavender, myrrh, orange, patchouli, sandalwood, vetiver or ylang ylang

Recipe: shamanic journey work wax melt

Whenever I do any shamanic work I always call in the trees to be with me to offer their strength, guidance, grounding and wisdom. Shamans work with trees to access the three worlds – the lower, middle and upper – so making a wax melt to work with these energies is a beautiful way to feel even more connected. I use just 1 g/0.03

oz of each and treat them with great reverence. Myrrh could also be used, but I like the combination of these three trees.

- ❊ 1 g/0.03 oz frankincense
- ❊ 1 g/0.03 oz palo santo (a very potent-smelling oil so you can use less)
- ❊ 1 g/0.03 oz sandalwood

Recipe: mental clarity wax melt

- ❊ 1 g/0.03 oz peppermint
- ❊ 1 g/0.03 oz rosemary
- ❊ 1 g/0.03 oz lemon

Recipe: space-cleansing wax melt

- ❊ use up to 3 g/0.1 oz of any of the following essential oils or combinations: basil, clove, lavender, lemon verbena, mint, palo santo, sage or white sage
- ❊ herbs and/or crystals of your choice

Recipe: basic herbal bath melt

For a variation on wax melts you can also make bath melts, luxurious herb bombs that melt in your bath, nourish your skin and allow you to sit with your intentions. You don't need wax for these ones, as you want them to melt away into the bath water.

EQUIPMENT/ INGREDIENTS

- a cauldron with a heat source or a double boiler
- mixing bowl
- a mould that can tolerate heat (I use silicone soap moulds, although little cauldron moulds would be cute! You can also use muffin liners in a muffin tray if you don't have a mould)
- ✖ 92 g/3.2 oz cocoa butter
- ✖ 22 g/0.7 oz infused oil such as sweet almond or jojoba

* 15 g/0.5 oz colloidal or whole ground oats
* 15 g/0.5 oz Epsom salts
* 3 g/0.1 oz green, pink or rhassoul clay for colour
* 3 g/0.1 oz of essential oil/s of your choice
* herbs of your choice
* pressed flowers to add to the finished product, optional

DIRECTIONS

1. Place the herbs into the mould and set aside.

2. Heat the cocoa butter and oil in a cauldron until they have both melted.

3. Remove from the heat and allow to cool a little.

4. While the mixture is cooling, combine the oats, Epsom salts and clay in the bowl.

5. Add the essential oils to the melted oils and stir well.

6. Pour the dry ingredients into the cauldron with the melted oils and stir until well combined.

7. Pour the mixture into the mould over the herbs. Pressed flowers look beautiful when added to the finished product, so if you wish to use some place them on top.

8. Place in the freezer until set.

9. Pop the shapes out of the mould and they are ready to use. Rub them all over your skin while in the bath and enjoy!

Note: sometimes melts can make your bath a little slippery, so take care when you're getting out of the bath.

On the following pages are some recipes that make great bath melts.

Recipe: a big warm hug

Are you filling your cup? Do you need some love and self-care? What better way to give back to yourself than a beautiful self-love bath. Not only could you use a bath melt, but you could also include bath salts and have a brew on hand to sip while in there next to your cauldron candle. Better yet, you know that you made everything yourself with pure intention, love and gratitude.

INGREDIENTS

* 92 g/3.2 oz cocoa butter
* 22 g/0.7 oz rose infused oil
* 15 g/0.5 oz oats
* 15 g/0.5 oz Epsom salts
* 3 g/0.1 oz pink clay
* 3 g/0.1 oz rose essential oil
* rose petals

DIRECTIONS

Follow the directions for the basic bath melt.

Recipe: de-stress bath melt

You know, I am the biggest fan of lavender. I use it for everything, although when I was younger I hated the smell and thought it was something only old people used. Thankfully, we grow up and come to appreciate everything more and now it is one of my go-to herbs. You don't always have to go with what's new and fashionable and I know lavender is a very sustainable plant so I will be using it for years to come. De-stress by letting that shit go!

* 92 g/3.2 oz cocoa butter
* 22 g/0.7 oz lavender-infused oil
* 15 g/0.5 oz oats
* 15 g/0.5 oz Epsom salts
* 3 g/0.1 oz kaolin clay
* 3 g/0.1 oz lavender essential oil

Recipe: FOREST bathing melt

- ✗ 92 g/3.2 oz cocoa butter
- ✗ 22 g/0.7 oz lavender-infused oil
- ✗ 15 g/0.5 oz Epsom salts
- ✗ 3 g/0.1 oz green clay
- ✗ 3 g/0.1 oz cedarwood and/or vetiver, Scots pine or silver fir essential oil

Recipe: Cerridwen's cauldron of sensuality

- ✗ 92 g3.2 oz cocoa butter
- ✗ 22 g0.7 oz rose- or vanilla-infused oil
- ✗ 15 g/0.5 oz oats
- ✗ 15 g/0.5 oz Epsom salts
- ✗ 3 g/0.1 oz pink clay
- ✗ 3 g/0.1 oz vanilla, sandalwood or orange essential oil
- ✗ rose petals, optional

CHAPTER 6

Fire magick

C auldrons are perfect to place fire in, because they are generally made from cast iron or ceramic. We can use charcoal blocks, candles and other burning items within them, and can even make the cauldron itself into a candle with crystals, herbs and spices with our intentions. They not only make beautiful altar items, they make truly special gifts when you set them with healing intentions.

CANDLES

Candle making is a large subject that could fill its own book, so I will keep this as simple as possible for those who are new to making candles. For the more experienced I hope this section gives you further ideas about what to make and what candles can be used for.

Cauldron candles are not only practical, they are also environmentally friendly and serve a great purpose on your altar. They create a beautiful environment, work with the fire elemental energy, can be made with specific intentions in mind and can encompass herbs and crystals you wish to work with. The vessel can be used over and over again, and each candle can be created with a different intention.

Altar-ready cauldron candles.

Safety precautions: *please note that in Australia for safety reasons there are laws that state that anything added to a candle that is flammable may only produce up to a five-second flame. We don't want to put a whole heap of flammable objects close to a flame, right? Exactly, so please ensure you have just a small amount of plant matter and that it is not placed too close to a flame. You will find that if you keep to this rule the plant matter will end up sinking into the wax and will only burn occasionally. Also be mindful when burning candles not to put them near a breeze or curtains or where animals or small children may knock or touch them. Be mindful of where you place them for everyone's safety.*

What you will need

I tend to stay away from using soy wax (processed soybean oil) because it can be related to deforestation, GMO-modified soybeans and the use of pesticides and other chemicals, something I encourage you to explore further. For these reasons I choose to use beeswax and support local suppliers.

The herbs used for incense can also be used in candle recipes, as they are able to be burned. I don't use fragrances in my candles because fragrances are synthetic, and if you use essential oils you need a very large amount, which I don't feel is a very sustainable practice unless you are growing and making the essential oils yourself or they come from a reputable grower or seller. I understand that people like things that smell pretty, but we also need to open ourselves up to the other qualities the candle holds and the intent it carries.

Wick for your vessel: you always have to ensure you purchase the right wick for the size of your vessel, because this affects the burn rate of the candle. If it is not large enough it will go out, and if it is too large the wick will burn quickly and create a sizeable flame. Therefore, it is essential for you to research and trial different types. Most candlewick suppliers have a guide for buying their wicks on their websites, so I haven't included a chart here. To get you started, though, you might like to get a 1 mm/0.03 in thick wick for a vessel that is around 5 cm/1 in in diameter. Beeswax is very different from soy wax in the way it burns, so always ensure you get wicks in the size that is required for beeswax.

Recipe: basic candle

This basic recipe will get you started. The addition of coconut oil to beeswax gives it a nice smooth texture.

EQUIPMENT/ INGREDIENTS

- a cauldron that will become the candle
- a double boiler using a Pyrex jug or a wax melter specifically for candle making (temperature controlled and with a spout for pouring the wax straight out of when melted)
- a wick to suit the vessel (specifically for beeswax)
- a clothes peg and a wick-holder stick or a bamboo skewer or pencil
- 450 g/16 oz beeswax (try sourcing this locally if possible)
- 50 g/1.7 oz coconut oil
- essential oil/s, optional
- herbs and crystals of choice, optional

Melting beeswax.

Secure wick.

DIRECTIONS

1. Put the beeswax in a heatproof jug and place it in a water bath on medium heat. Alternatively, place the wax into a wax melter.

2. Place the wick inside the cauldron you intend to become the candle. Some wicks come with little metal holders on the bottom so when you pour in the wax it doesn't move, so if there is one this needs to be stuck to the bottom. Some use double-sided sticker dots to keep them down or you can use a little dob of glue. I use larger metal holders that don't require anything to hold them on the bottom and pour the wax in very slowly so the wick doesn't move.

Altar-ready cauldron candle.

3. Secure the top of the wick at the top of the vessel by either tying it around a bamboo skewer or pencil or through the hole in the wick holder stick then secure with a peg. If it is a thick wick it may not need a peg to secure it.

4. Once the wax has melted, add the coconut oil and combine well.

5. If you are using essential oils add them to the mix when it has cooled down a little, as they can be destroyed by heat. You also need to stir them in really well.

6. Slowly pour the mixture into the cauldron and fill to close to the top of the vessel, leaving some room for the herbs and crystals.

7. When the wax has cooled and you can see it is changing colour as it hardens you can arrange the plant matter and crystals on top. You might need to push them in a little so they stick. Alternatively, if the wax is too hard you can heat the top with a hairdryer and then place your items in the wax. I tend to place the big things in before they set and then leave the little things until the end.

Colouring candle wax

Colour can play a big role in a candle's purpose and there are many ways you can add colour to the wax. If you choose to colour the beeswax choose natural colourants, usually spices such as turmeric, paprika, cinnamon and charcoal. You could also infuse the coconut oil with a herb that has colour, so experiment a little and do some testers beforehand. Colours should be added when the wax is melted and stirred in well to make sure it doesn't sink to the bottom.

* * *

Using the basic candle recipe method, you might like to try the following candle variations.

LOVE CAULDRON CANDLE

What brings the feeling of love to you: is it roses, the colour pink or the smell of chocolate? If you want to bring love into your life you must first emanate that feeling, so let's bring in the feeling of love to a candle. You could choose from:

* Herbs: bougainvillea, cacao, catnip, chamomile, cinnamon, clove, dragon's blood resin, frankincense resin or essential oil, hibiscus flowers, nutmeg, rose petals, rosebuds, vanilla, vervain or ylang ylang.
* Crystals: rose quartz and pink stones.

VISIONARY AND DIVINATION CAULDRON CANDLE

When you think of visionary or divination what comes to mind?

* Herbs: mugwort is my go-to herb for these types of recipes, but feel free to use other herbs such as eyebright, lavender or yarrow.

× Crystals: I like the addition of amethyst crystals to help connect with my third eye and spiritual guides. Lavender and amethyst are both purple, and look beautiful together. Quartz crystal might also be a good choice here.

SACRED CEREMONY CANDLE

Even though every ceremony is sacred, sometimes you feel like adding something a little extra special to your ritual. Choose something that honours the sacred plant spirits that you use at special times to bring a high-vibrational purity to your space.

× Herbs: copal resin, frankincense, palo santo or white sage.
× Crystals: white or clear quartz.

CELTIC CAULDRON CANDLE

Use this candle to call in the energies of the Celtic other worlds or for rituals where you wish to contact the fae and perform shamanic visionary work. Choose any herbs or crystals that you wish to work with, and if you physically can't acquire some you can inscribe their corresponding Ogham symbol if they have one (see Appendix III) into the wax surface.

× Herbs: apple seeds or twigs, blackberry, birch, elder (flowers), fern, gorse, hawthorn, hazelnut, oak (acorn), pussy willow, rowan, Scots pine or silver fir.
× Crystals: crystals that always come to mind when I am working with Celtic energies include dark green crystals (for a connection with nature), staurolite (fairy cross) and fairy stones (menalite), or you could also use stones or pebbles from the UK or Ireland such as my favourite Preseli bluestone.

PASSING OVER CANDLE

As hard as it can be when someone we love passes over, there are beautiful rituals we can do to honour their presence in our lives and show our gratitude by creating beautiful spirit medicines to help with their transition. For those times that you are with them and you know they are about to pass over you might like to burn a candle during the process, or you can honour them by burning it after they pass or at their grave.

 ✷ Herbs: aspen, blackthorn, borage, cypress essential oil, heather, marshmallow, motherwort, nettle, oak, patchouli, vetiver or the yew Ogham symbol (Appendix III).

MULLEIN OR HAG TORCH

Mullein is an amazing herb although it is classed as a weed in many places. Not only is it medicinal, the flower stalks can be dried and turned into mullein or hag torches. They are generally used for outdoor purposes as the flame can be big and they can be adorned with many more herbs during the final stage of making them.

I have chosen to grow mullein and it has been a truly rewarding experience. The species I grow, *Verbascum thapsus,* reaches 2.5 m/8 ft tall when flowering (it flowers in its second year), but there are smaller varieties. You can harvest the leaves, dry them and use them as tea or infuse them to make oil. Once the flowers have bloomed you let the stalks dry completely then cut them off; the stalks are what you use for the candles. You might want to give the plant a shake so the seeds can fall to the ground to make new ones the following year.

Recipe: mullein torch

EQUIPMENT

- A fairly large cauldron or Pyrex jug to melt the wax in or a wax melter, which is a great investment if you wish to make a lot of candles and some even look like cauldrons! Don't worry if the stalk doesn't completely fit in, as you can use a spoon to pour the wax over the stalk to cover it.

A drying rack on which to place the candles to dry. This could be as simple as some baking paper or a steel rack from the oven, or you can make something that the stalks can be stood up in so the candles aren't lying flat.

If you wish to add rose petals, lavender or something else to the candle on the last dip, have that ready on a flat tray as you will roll them over it. Baking paper is a good option here.

DIRECTIONS

1. Heat the beeswax in the cauldron or Pyrex jug.

2. Add any colourings and stir well.

3. The rest is easy: you just dip the stalk into the melted beeswax until it is lightly covered, making sure you leave a part uncovered to hold. This is the part you will stick in the ground when lit. Place the stalk on the rack to dry.

4. Once dry, repeat the process over and over until there is a nice thick coat. On the last coat and while the wax is still warm, roll it in the mix of herbs if you have chosen to coat it.

5. To light the torch, cut the top off and light the centre stalk, which is essentially the wick.

Lit mullein torch.

INCENSE

There are many herbs and spices you can use for incense, and I always suggest making them with items you already have to start with. When you know what you are doing you can branch out. Many dried herbs, resins and woods are available online, so you need to either have an intent on what you want to make so you can choose the appropriate herb, or trust your intuition and use what you have or grow in your garden.

Incense can be added to a charcoal disk inside a cauldron, or you can mix the ingredients in the cauldron and add your magic to them as you combine them for later use. I like to use bamboo charcoal as it is free of toxic ingredients and doesn't burn as hot, so it won't scorch the other ingredients. Japanese incense suppliers are great for all these beautiful tools and ingredients. Suggested herbs you might like to get started with include:

✘ bay leaves for manifestation, clairvoyance, purification, to heighten intuition, ward off negative energy and relieve anxiety and stress

✘ cinnamon to increase psychic ability, attract wealth, healing and protection

- clove for protection, cleansing, love and money
- copal resin for protection, cleansing and purifying
- dragon's blood resin for love, sexual energy and protection
- frankincense resin for consecration, protection, healing, love and lifting vibration
- lavender for meditation, relaxing, protection and cleansing
- lemon peel for moon magick, purification and love
- myrrh resin for healing, protection, consecration and peace
- mugwort for visionary or divination work
- nutmeg to increase psychic abilities and spiritual connection, banishing, reveal truth, love, luck, money and confidence
- orange peel for love, luck and wealth
- palo santo wood for cleansing, grounding, sacredness and transformation
- rosemary, the memory herb to help with cleansing and protection
- sage for healing and cleansing
- sandalwood for spiritual healing and uplifting and protection
- thyme for protection, courage, strength, manifestation, purification, sound sleep, healing, magick and love
- white sage for cleansing, protection, wisdom and clarity.

If you define what you want your incense to be for, you can then create combinations based on what is readily available or easy to acquire. Below are some combinations you might like to try for specific purposes:

- ceremony and ritual: consecrating, cleansing and spiritually uplifting herbs such as myrrh, palo santo, white sage, frankincense and copal
- protection and deflecting: bay leaf, dragon's blood, clove, nutmeg, sandalwood and white sage
- calm and peace: lavender and myrrh

- ✖ love: clove, dragon's blood, nutmeg, orange and rose
- ✖ abundance and gratitude: palo santo, sandalwood and white sage
- ✖ moon magick: lemon, mugwort, myrrh, sandalwood and turmeric
- ✖ meditation: think grounding herbs such as tree barks and resins, visionary herbs such as mugwort, yarrow and cinnamon and calming herbs such as lavender.

Notes: if you are using resin for incense it needs to be ground to a powder. You can buy it already ground, which I highly recommend, or you can grind it in a mortar and pestle. If you use an electric grinder the resin can be either too hard and wreck the blender or become very sticky and hard to get off the blades. I suggest freezing the resin and blades if you can before trying to process it. Many Chinese herb grinders or hammer mills can do the job as they are specifically made for Chinese herbs, which can be very tough.

If you are using woods I recommend you use a chisel to break the wood down to small pieces the size of a grain of rice, which is fine for loose incense, or you then put them in a blender to reduce them down to a powder for combustible incense. Coffee grinders can be a good option.

Loose, non-combustible incense

This is the easiest to make and only requires the ingredients to be the size of a grain of rice and smaller. You can use tree barks, resins and herbs. You could either purchase dried herbs or grow your own and you can use one herb or a combination of herbs, resins and woods. That's really all there is to it. All you need is a blender or the ability to grind your herbs or plants down to a small-enough size.

This type of incense needs a burner of some sort, so you can use charcoal disks in the cauldron or you could use an incense warmer such as a mica plate, which are great for resins and wood as they don't physically burn the incense so the scents are very pure.

Method 1: burning loose incense on a charcoal disk

EQUIPMENT/INGREDIENTS

- A small, cast-iron cauldron will work best for this as the charcoal gets extremely hot. Alternatively, you can put sand or ash in the cauldron and place the charcoal disk on top if you are using ceramic, copper or brass so it doesn't damage the cauldron. It's also good to have a lid in case you need to extinguish the fire or smoke quickly.
- a charcoal disk (I use the Baieido brand)
- loose incense

DIRECTIONS

1. Place the sand or ash in the cauldron if necessary and light the charcoal disk. These can take a while, so ensure it is properly lit before placing it in your cauldron. Sprinkle enough of the loose incense on top of the burning charcoal to burn but not smother it.

2. Add more loose incense to the disk as necessary.

Method 2: heating loose incense on a mica plate

A Japanese method of heating loose incense is on top of a mica plate, which heats the incense but doesn't burn it and imparts different notes as it heats. This is a beautiful experience if you really want to take the time to be present with your practice, and using a cauldron is absolutely perfect for this.

EQUIPMENT/INGREDIENTS

- small cauldron
- ash or white rice ash (can readily be bought online)
- charcoal disk
- mica plate
- loose incense

DIRECTIONS

1. Fill the cauldron to about 1.5 cm/0.5 in from the top with the ash and pat it down nice and flat.

2. Push the charcoal disk into the ash to make an indent of it.

3. Pull the charcoal disk out, light it and place it back in the indent. When you know it is completely lit, place a fine layer of ash over the top of it.

4. Put the mica plate on top of the lit charcoal.

5. Add the loose incense on top of the mica plate and enjoy.

Another way of burning loose incense on a mica plate or incense warmer is to knead it together with honey. Traditionally, plums were used. The loose incense needs to be a very fine powder first. Roll the powder and honey into balls or compress it into small flowers or other shapes, and store them until they harden and the scents mature.

Method 3: using a makko trail

You can use a makko trail to burn incense. Makko powder enables loose incense to burn, much like a charcoal disk. Makko trails are very meditative and can last hours.

EQUIPMENT/INGREDIENTS

- small cauldron
- white rice ash
- makko powder
- stick incense
- loose incense

DIRECTIONS

1. Fill the cauldron to about 1.5 cm/0.5 in from the top with the rice ash and pat it down nice and flat.

2. Make a small indented line in the ash and put the makko powder into the dent.

3. Place a small piece of stick incense at the start of the makko trail and light it; this will light the makko trail.

4. Add the loose incense on top of the makko and enjoy.

Method 4: incense trails

Brass incense stencil.

You can get brass incense stencils that help lay a line of finely powdered loose incense on top of the rice ash without the need for makko powder. These used to be a form of timekeeper in China, as certain trails would take a particular time to burn. Try making your own Celtic-themed stencils. These take a while to get the hang of, so adding some makko powder to the loose incense can help.

EQUIPMENT/INGREDIENTS

- small cauldron
- white rice ash
- brass stencil
- loose incense

DIRECTIONS

1. Fill the cauldron to about 1.5 cm/0.5 in from the top with the rice ash and pat it down flat.

2. Put the stencil on top and carefully place the incense over the trail holes, making sure you don't overfill it and don't compress it. You want a healthy air flow in there.

3. Carefully remove the stencil without breaking the incense trail.

4. Light the trail with an incense stick and enjoy.

Combustible incense

Making combustible incense requires loose incense that is as fine a powder as possible and a binder and/or ingredient to make it burn such as makko powder. I like to make small, thin incense sticks for use at my altar each morning that are made from home-grown plants. I make lavender, rosemary or white sage sticks that are simply my ground-up herb with a small amount of xanthan gum added. Because I make them very small in size I don't need to add makko.

If you want a natural binder you can use marshmallow root, guar gum, xanthan gum or honey; you only need ⅛ teaspoon binder per 2 tablespoons of plant matter. I also like to use a clay extruder, which can be readily found online and in pottery supply shops, which helps to get an even size of incense without having to hand roll it.

Feel free to mix the herbs once you know what they smell like when they are burning on their own, as they sometimes don't smell like you think they would. You might want to make the incense using one herb to connect with that herb each time or make a mix of herbs that works best for your intention. Prepare a small batch to start with, let it dry and then light it to see if the smell is nice before making a big batch.

The beautiful thing about making combustible incense, just like smudging, is it really incorporates the five elements: we use plants from the earth, water to bind it, fire to light it and air to fuel it and we create the spirit connection with the plant. You could also do this with loose incense by putting sand in a shell as the water element and placing the charcoal in there for the incense to burn on.

Recipe: **basic combustible incense sticks**

EQUIPMENT/INGREDIENTS

- cauldron
- spoon
- extruder with a small to medium hole attachment
- water spray bottle (you can use water or hydrosols that have no additives, or incorporate the water from a herbal simmer or tea)
- tray or plate for the finished incense to dry on (baking paper is also good to use)
- ✹ herb/s or plant matter of your choice
- ✹ binder of your choice such as marshmallow root, guar gum, xanthan gum or honey

DIRECTIONS

1. Place the herbs or plant matter in the cauldron, add the binder and mix well. Start with 1 tablespoon and a pinch of binder if you are making your first one.

2. Spray a little water or hydrosol into the mix and stir. The mixture should be moist enough to stick together but not saturated, so add a small amount of water each time.

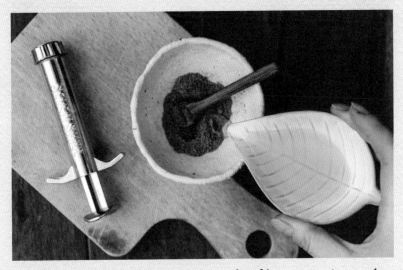

3. Pick up some of the mixture and softly squeeze it together. You should be able to see when it sticks together and forms a mass that doesn't separate. Don't squeeze it too hard, as you want some air in there so it burns nice and evenly.

4. Roll the mixture into a cylinder that will fit into the extruder. Hold your finger over the hole so the mixture doesn't squirt out and push the end a bit to get it all down without any gaps.

5. Slowly extrude the incense onto the tray or baking paper, keeping the lines as straight as you can. Make them the length of your tray and then cut them to the size you like; I cut them to around 5 cm/2 in long. You can straighten them out and roll them a little with your fingers to compress them more if needed.

6. Let the sticks completely dry before lighting, which usually takes a day or two.

Troubleshooting: if the stick doesn't burn for long before going out it may either be too thick or compacted or you may have used too much binder. The great thing is you just need to grind down the stick into a powder again, add what you need and remodel it. If the stick falls apart or breaks, try adding more binder or making them a little thicker.

For further information on making incense with makko powder you might like to refer to my book *Plant Spirit Medicine*.

MANIFESTING, RELEASING AND CUTTING CORDS

Recipe: bay-leaf burning for manifestation

Bay leaves have long been burned as smudge and incense, and for manifestation. This quick manifestation technique can be done with minimal preparation and fuss. Make sure you are close to an open window or door.

EQUIPMENT

- cauldron that can tolerate fire inside it (preferably with a lid in case you need to extinguish the fire immediately)
- candle for inside the cauldron, optional
- lighter
- bay leaf
- pen to write your intention on the leaf

DIRECTIONS

1. Light the candle and place it inside the cauldron if you are using one.

2. Set your intention for what you wish to manifest, feeling it as though you already have it and being grateful for it. Emotion and intention are key.

3. Write what you wish to manifest on the bay leaf and ask the bay leaf plant spirit to help you manifest your desire.

4. Place the bay leaf in the flame of the candle or a lighter, then place the whole leaf in the cauldron. Allow the smoke to blow away into the ether through an open window.

Recipe: INTENTION RELEASING/ CORD CUTTING

Dear past...

Spells, petitions and intentions have long been burned in cauldrons. This technique is just like the bay-leaf burning except that you write the spell, petition or intention on paper. You can also write on the paper whatever you want to let go of or cut a cord to. This is not a negative thing; in fact, it's quite the opposite as it represents standing up for yourself and saying you no longer allow certain influences to have any control over you. It can be incredibly effective because it comes from your intention to remove something from your life, which means you are ready to move forward.

EQUIPMENT

- cauldron that can tolerate fire inside it (preferably with a lid in case you need to extinguish the fire immediately)
- candle for inside the cauldron, optional
- lighter
- paper and pen

DIRECTIONS

1. Light the candle and place it inside the cauldron if you are using one.

2. Set your intention for what you wish to let go of, feeling it as though you are really ready to let go of whatever is holding you back from moving forward. Emotion and intention are key.

3. Write what you wish to let go of on the piece of paper.

4. Place the paper in the flame of the candle or a lighter and let it burn in the cauldron. As it burns, feel the weight lifting from you and gratitude flowing in for allowing yourself to let go.

5. Allow the smoke to blow away into the ether through an open window.

Recipe: CAULDRON SPIRIT FIRE

Cast-iron cauldrons are perfect to use spirit fire in. Essentially, you infuse rubbing alcohol with fragrant herbs such as lavender, mint, rosemary and white sage, although any herb will be suitable if you wish to use it for its specific properties. When you place it in your cauldron and light it, it will steadily burn and then go out. You can use it for setting alight your intentions or spells or even to do some fire divination.

DIRECTIONS

1. Place your chosen herbs or plants in a preserving jar and cover with rubbing alcohol.
2. Give it a shake and let it sit somewhere for two weeks, giving it a further shake once a day.
3. Strain the herbs and place the alcohol in a safe container.

To use, place a small amount of the liquid in your cauldron and light it with a long match or gas lighter.

Chapter 7

Magickal meals

In the kitchen and cooking in a cauldron takes us back to our ancestral roots, where everything happened in the home and the hearth was the centre of the household. It was where the family would not only gather in front of the fire, but could sit and watch the food cooking over it. Nowadays we have so many kitchen gadgets that speed up the process and allow us more time to do other things, so when cooking magickal meals I would like to bring your attention back to being mindful and present when cooking. What ingredients are you putting into your meals and how are you honouring them? Do you cook for a specific intention or purpose, or would you like to become more aware in the kitchen, make it less a chore and put more love and soul into your creations? Be present when you are cooking and have an intention, whether that is just pouring love or comfort into it or something bigger. The same goes for when you eat the food you have prepared: be present and honour your co-creation.

We also know how tasty food is when you're camping, so why not take a tripod and cauldron or camp oven to use over the campfire?

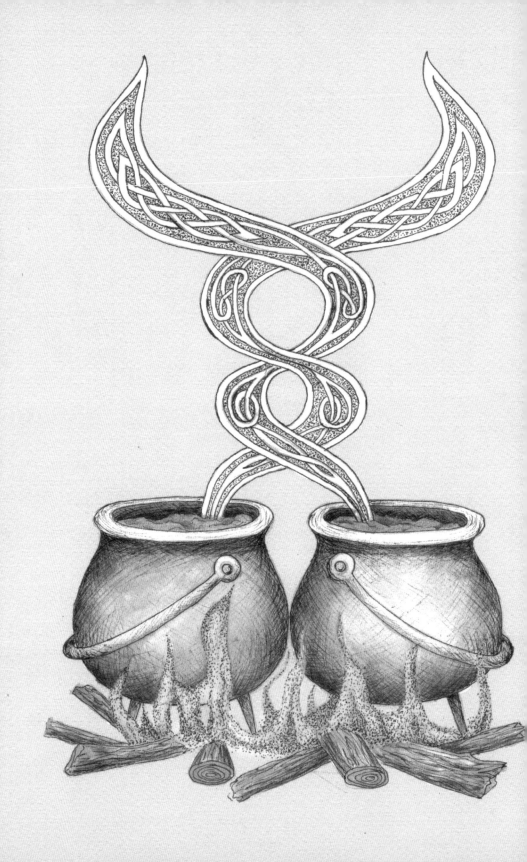

DAMPER

Cauldron damper.

Damper is a good old Australian outback recipe that is most suited to a camp oven or cauldron when you are outdoors or camping. The great thing about damper is you only need three ingredients to make it: flour, water and a pinch of salt. The other great thing about damper is it tastes amazing with butter and golden or maple syrup and you can put anything you like in it, so if you like savoury you can add cheese, bacon, rosemary and salt. It's up to you!

The trick to making good damper is not kneading the dough, because this pushes the air out of it. You can make it in a Dutch oven in your kitchen, in a cauldron, or in a camp oven outdoors. If you are making it over a campfire you don't place the cauldron directly over the flames; cooking is best done over hot coals or charcoal. You can use heat beads as well, which make it easier to manage. The cauldron needs to be moved off to the side of the fire and placed on top of a few hot coals that you have taken from the fire. You also place some hot coals on top of the lid. You don't want too much heat, although the lower the heat the longer it will take to cook. How many coals you will need will be dependent on how big the cauldron is. It might take a bit of trial and error, and you can lift the lid while the damper is cooking to see how it is going. You don't need to preheat the cauldron before placing the damper in: just whack it straight on the heat and cover the top. It usually takes between 30 minutes to 1 hour to cook depending on the size of the dough and of the cauldron.

Alternatively, you can place your cauldron on top of a griddle or wire rack over a fire pit if the fire isn't too big. I suggest you place a trivet covered in aluminium foil in the bottom of the cooking vessel so the damper doesn't burn on the bottom, but you can make it without this as long as you ensure you don't have too many coals under the cauldron. The best thing about cast iron is that the heat is evenly distributed around the pot.

Making damper in the kitchen oven is obviously a lot easier, but there is something special about cooking a sumptuous damper outside in your cauldron!

Recipe: basic damper

EQUIPMENT/INGREDIENTS

- cast-iron cauldron, camp oven or Dutch oven
- trivet wrapped in aluminium foil with a scatter of flour on top, optional
- mixing bowl

- 2 cups self-raising flour
- pinch of salt
- ¾ cup of water (you might not need all of it)

DIRECTIONS

1. Combine the flour and salt in the mixing bowl.
2. Add the water slowly and mix with a butter knife, using only as much water as you need to form a firm dough.
3. Don't knead the dough: just use your hands to bring the mixture together to form a nice round ball shape that's flattened on the bottom.
4. Put the trivet inside the cauldron and place the dough on top of the trivet or straight into the cauldron if you are not using the trivet after adding a little oil to it. Put the lid on the cauldron and place over the hot coals next to the fire, add a few more coals to the lid and sit back and wait for it to cook. Check on it after 20 minutes and then keep checking on it until it is golden and cooked through.
5. Enjoy it with your choice of spread by the fire.

Recipe: damper scones

Damper scones are very similar to plain damper except you add butter to the recipe. These are smaller and won't take long to cook, say around 12 minutes depending on what size you make them.

EQUIPMENT/INGREDIENTS

- cast-iron cauldron, camp oven or Dutch oven
- trivet wrapped in aluminium foil with a scatter of flour on top, optional
- chopping board
- mixing bowl
- butter knife

* 2 cups self-raising flour
* 55 g/2 oz of butter
* ¾ cup of water (you might not need all of it)
* pinch of salt

DIRECTIONS

1. Combine the flour and salt in the mixing bowl.

2. Rub the flour and butter together with your fingertips until the mixture resembles breadcrumbs.

3. Add the water slowly and mix with the knife, using only as much water as you need to form a firm dough: not too wet and not too dry. Don't knead the dough: just use your hands to bring the mixture together.

4. Lightly dust the chopping board with flour, place the dough on top and divide it into six equal pieces.

5. Form the pieces into balls, then place them inside the cauldron with a little oil or on the trivet if you are using one. Put the lid on and place the cauldron over hot coals next to a fire. Add a few more coals to the lid and sit back and wait for the scones to cook. Check on them after 20 minutes and keep checking until they are cooked through.

6. Enjoy by the fire with your choice of spread.

RECIPE VARIATIONS

Here are some ideas for other things you might like to add to your damper or scones when they are cooked.

INGREDIENTS

- ✖ bacon, cheese and onion
- ✖ rosemary, garlic and salt
- ✖ sultanas and cinnamon (my favourite!)

CONDIMENTS

- ✖ strawberry or raspberry jam
- ✖ cream
- ✖ butter
- ✖ maple or golden syrup.

BREAD

Dutch oven bread.

Bread is very similar to damper: you just need a couple of extra ingredients and to let the dough rise. Bread can be made in a Dutch oven in the kitchen. I have fallen in love with my Dutch oven and can't believe I only bought my first one in my late 40s! There is something so gratifying about making food in it and it just feels so homely. It really is a kitchen cauldron in many aspects. Now, I am by no means a master chef, so feel free to create your own bread recipe. Once I have a good recipe I like to stick to it.

Recipe: basic bread

I love simplicity and this recipe is just that: it's a no-knead, no-fuss recipe that takes next to no time to make. Plus, once you get the hang of it you can mix it up and add whatever you like to it.

EQUIPMENT/ INGREDIENTS

- Dutch oven
- mixing bowls
- baking paper
- 3 cups of flour
- 1½ cups room-temperature water
- 1 tsp active dry yeast
- ¾ tsp salt

DIRECTIONS

1. Combine the yeast and water in a bowl and leave it to sit for 15 minutes. The yeast should foam a little on the top.

2. Combine the flour and salt in a separate mixing bowl.

3. Add the water mix to the flour. Don't work it too much; just ensure it is combined.

4. Cover and leave to sit for 8 to 24 hours in a warm environment to give it time to rise.

5. When ready to bake, preheat the kitchen oven to 230°C/450°F and put the Dutch oven inside.

6. Sprinkle flour on a flat surface and gently fold the dough into the centre a few times until it is coated with flour and forms a ball.

7. Put the dough ball on top of the baking paper and then inside the Dutch oven once the oven is at the correct temperature.

8. Cover and bake for 30 minutes. You can then either remove the lid and bake for another 15–20 minutes or keep the lid on for the entire cooking period. I like to keep the lid on to prevent the dough from getting too dark on the top. This also keeps the moisture in. The bread is ready when it is brown on top and lifts easily from the Dutch oven.

9. Carefully lift out with the baking paper and place on a cooling rack for up to 1 hour before serving. You can eat it straight away if you like hot bread!

Recipe: ROSEMARY and salt bread

If you like you can add additional ingredients when you fold the dough, such as 2 tablespoons of rosemary and 1 teaspoon of salt. These are so beautiful in combination, but feel free to trial your own mix. I also sprinkle some rosemary leaves and salt on top just before it goes into the oven.

Recipe: CINNAMON and sultana bread

For this bread I substitute the plain flour with spelt flour and add 3 teaspoons of cinnamon and ¾ cup of sultanas. I find that when I make it with spelt flour the mix is very wet and doesn't form a ball, but it still cooks fine. This bread tastes great sliced and toasted with butter.

STEW

The well-known stew is one of the most ancient recipes for cauldrons: this is exactly what our ancestors ate from them. They can be so varied and there are many recipes out there for them and nothing beats it after a long day outside. I recommend looking up camp-oven stew or potjie recipes before your next camping trip and making up a beautiful dinner. Damper goes perfectly with these to soak up the juices, so you could make one beforehand or in a separate cauldron.

Recipe: basic stew

EQUIPMENT/ INGREDIENTS

- camp oven or cast-iron cauldron
- tripod or stand
- heavy-duty leather gloves or thick pot mitts (your cauldron will get extremely hot!)
- 1 kg beef, cut into cubes
- 2 carrots, chopped
- 3 potatoes, chopped
- 2 onions
- 4 garlic cloves, chopped
- 2 tbs mixed herbs such as rosemary, oregano, sage or thyme
- 3 bay leaves
- salt and pepper
- olive oil
- cornflour
- 2 beef stock cubes or 1 tbs bone broth
- water

DIRECTIONS

1. You need to get the cauldron or camp oven hot enough to fry the onions and garlic and brown the meat, so you can either take some coals from a fire and put them to the side to place the cauldron on top of or have a tripod to go over some coals

or the flame of the fire. You only need heat on the bottom of the vessel for stews.

2. Coat the beef in a thin layer of cornflour and set aside.

3. Add a big dollop of olive oil to the cauldron and allow it to get hot.

4. Put the onions in the cauldron and cook until they are nearly transparent.

5. Add the garlic and herbs and stir over the heat for 1 minute.

6. Add the beef and cook until it is well browned, then add the remaining vegetables and bay leaves.

7. Add the beef stock cubes and enough water to cover everything, and give it a good stir. Season with the salt and pepper.

8. Cook for a few hours, stirring regularly, over low heat. You will need to check that the stew is not boiling too fast as it may lose moisture too quickly or burn onto the bottom. When you are new to cauldron cooking it's best to keep an eye on it all the time to understand the heat and distance the cauldron needs to be from the flames.

CHOCOLATE CAULDRONS

There's no way we can do a cooking section and not mention chocolate, right? I love dark chocolate, not only for its taste and amazing health benefits but because I had the most amazing experience with the cacao plant spirit during a cacao ceremony. Whenever I work with chocolate I honour this spirit I met and only make the purest of chocolate products or drinks that I can.

The awesome part about having a fondue pot as a cauldron to cook with is that they are made for melting chocolate in, but you can also use a normal cauldron. You can even buy mini ceramic chocolate fondue sets that use a tealight for the heat source, which is very handy because they are little. I like to use fruit or nuts in my chocolate fondue: strawberries, almonds and hazelnuts are my favourites and the occasional goji berry. When you are working with nuts you can call in tree energy and hazel has always been the tree of knowledge according to the Celts – just as strawberries are synonymous with love.

There are two methods for making chocolate cauldrons.

Method 1: double boiler

Melt chocolate in a double boiler, dip the ingredients in and place them on a baking tray to cool. Any remaining chocolate will harden and can be kept for later use. I use this method to create magickal food for others or myself that can be stored in the fridge, so they can be made ahead of time.

Method 2: fondue

Create a chocolate fondue basic recipe, where the chocolate is mixed with cream so it remains fairly runny. These creations generally get eaten straight away. Fondues using this method are good if you are in ceremony with two or more people.

Note: it is best to use as dark a chocolate as possible: 70 per cent cacao or above is perfect or you can use ceremonial-grade cacao. If you really need to sweeten it a little try adding a touch of honey or maple syrup.

Method 1 recipe: chocolate love bombs

These have to be the easiest of the recipes. Strawberries dipped in chocolate: yes, please! Sometimes simplicity is key. When we remember that working with cacao is sacred, dipping a strawberry into it and honouring it brings you into a deeper connection with it. Learning from cacao allows us to open our hearts and gain guidance when we need it. These are great Valentine's treats with a loved one, or simply for when you are sitting in ritual alone and bringing in the love element. Be present and treat yourself.

EQUIPMENT/INGREDIENTS

- double-boiler cauldron
- mixing bowl
- baking tray lined with baking paper
- fork
- chocolate, as dark as possible (Lindt 70 per cent or above is lovely, but I also use ceremonial grade cacao, of which you only need a little bit – just enough to coat however many strawberries you have)
- strawberries, washed and patted dry
- maple syrup, optional

DIRECTIONS

1. Put some boiling water into the cauldron and return to the boil. Put the chocolate or cacao in the mixing bowl and then over the boiling water.

2. Stir until the chocolate melts while being present and calling in the cacao spirit to work with you. Add a dash of maple syrup if you wish and stir to combine.

3. Dip the strawberries into the melting chocolate with the fork or by holding the stems, calling on the spirit of the strawberries to be present.

4. Place on the baking tray to cool. These are best eaten on the day they are made.

Method 1 recipe: chocolate knowledge bites

Too often we just eat things without any thought about where they come from. Chocolate hazelnut bites are the perfect combination of working with two trees at once and they also taste awesome, which is a bonus. If you need any sweetener add a touch of pure maple syrup, then you will have the qualities of three trees in your recipe. I love working with tree medicine! These keep for ages in a sealed jar and are great before doing ritual work, meditating or study.

EQUIPMENT/ INGREDIENTS

- double-boiler cauldron
- mixing bowl
- baking tray lined with baking paper
- hazelnuts (best when roasted, but it is not essential)
- chocolate (enough to coat however many hazelnuts you have)
- maple syrup, optional

DIRECTIONS

1. To roast the hazelnuts, place them on a baking tray in a preheated oven at 180°C/360°F and bake for 10 minutes or until the skins crack and the nuts are aromatic. Remove the skins by placing the nuts in a tea towel and rubbing them together.

2. Place some boiling water in the cauldron and return to the boil. Put the chocolate in the mixing bowl then over the boiling water.

3. Stir until the chocolate melts while being present and calling in the cacao spirit to work with you. Add a dash of maple syrup if you wish and stir to combine.

4. Add the hazelnuts to the melted chocolate and roll them around to coat them.

5. Remove the hazelnuts from the cauldron and place them on the baking tray to cool. You can space them out in individual bites, or if you have melted too much chocolate you can spread the mixture out as a layer on the tray and when it cools break it into pieces.

6. Once cooled and set you can place the chocolate knowledge bites in a sealed glass jar.

Method 2 recipe: chocolate fondue

Chocolate fondue recipes are similar to the melted chocolate recipes except you won't need a double-boiler cauldron for them because we add the magick ingredient – cream – to the recipe, which prevents the chocolate from burning. The ritual or ceremony of eating with a group of friends or one on one and sharing love, support and laughter is an incredibly healing and uplifting experience.

Every meal we make, whether big or small, can be an opportunity to work our magick, because not only do our ingredients hold a specific vibration but so too can we instil our own magick into our food. What is the specific medicine you bring to the kitchen? Do you put your love and healing into your food?

EQUIPMENT/INGREDIENTS

- fondue pot or cauldron with a heat source
- ½ cup heavy cream
- 110 g/4 oz chocolate, chopped
- 1 tsp vanilla extract
- things to dip in the chocolate such as strawberries, raspberries, blueberries, banana, mango, pineapple, apple, figs, nuts, marshmallows, pretzels or popcorn

DIRECTIONS

When it comes to which foods to use for dipping I like to keep things natural, but it is up to you: sometimes we all need to indulge.

1. Place the cream in the fondue pot or cauldron and bring to a simmer. You can do this in a saucepan and transfer the cream to a cauldron or other vessel.

2. Gradually add the chocolate and stir until it is melted.

3. Add the vanilla extract and stir through.

4. Enjoy dipping in your fruits and nuts, savouring each bite and be present!

MULLED WINE

What's this, you say: mulled wine is magickal? How could it not be, I say! After all, it has red wine, oranges, cinnamon, star anise and cloves, which all have their own spiritual qualities: protection, love, healing and wealth. It's also a beautiful drink to have on a nice cold night with friends around a campfire in your cauldron. Mulled wine can be made in a slow cooker, cauldron, large fondue pot or Dutch oven.

Recipe: basic mulled wine

INGREDIENTS

- ✖ 1 bottle red wine (Merlot or Grenache are best)
- ✖ 2 small or 1 large peeled fresh orange (love, luck, wealth)
- ✖ 2 cinnamon sticks (increases psychic ability, attracts wealth, healing, protection)
- ✖ 3 star anise, whole (cord cutting, protection)
- ✖ 4 cloves, whole (protection, cleansing, love, money)
- ✖ ¼ cup brandy, Cointreau or port, optional
- ✖ 1–2 tbs maple syrup or honey, optional

DIRECTIONS

1. Juice half the orange, slice the other half into rounds and place them in the cauldron.

2. Add the remaining ingredients and stir well. You can leave the sweetener out until last if you want to see what it's like without it first.

3. Heat the mix very gently: you don't want it to boil or bubble but just to warm up.

4. You can cook the mixture for anywhere between 15 minutes and 3 hours, but know that the longer you heat it the spicier it will become and sometimes it can end up quite bitter.

Serve warm by pouring into heatproof glasses, adding a little slice of orange or star anise for aesthetics.

There are so many ways we can incorporate magick into our food and when we share it with friends there is a coming together of similar energy. Let your imagination guide you on how you can incorporate magickal meals prepared in a cauldron into your daily life or special events.

CHAPTER 8

Miscellaneous magick

SPIRIT OR SPELL BOTTLES

The process of making spirit or spell bottles is a really easy one and it can bring great change. Essentially, they are a mix of herbs, crystals, oils, essences, shells or feathers – practically anything you can think of. You can keep the spirit bottle on your altar or wherever you feel you will need it, such as on your desk or in your car. They not only serve as a reminder of your intent, but they also carry the energies of all the items you place inside them. When you pick up the bottle and hold it to your heart you call in the energies to help you with your intention.

Again and as always, your intention is key. If, for instance, you want something to help you feel calm when you are anxious you might like to select herbs such as lavender, chamomile, valerian or California poppy. You might like to add some small crystals to the mix such as black tourmaline to help ground you, black onyx to deflect energy or a small amount of dirt from your home to feel close to it when you are away. You want to use items that work together in this way.

Method: basic spirit bottle

DIRECTIONS

1. Gather all the items you wish to use together, including a bottle or jar of some sort. I find small ones I can fit in the palm of my hand perfect, or you can purchase small glass bottle necklaces that you can wear if you don't have a medicine pouch to place the items in.

2. Create your ritual or ceremony, cleanse your area and have your cauldron ready to mix everything together. Alternatively, you can place each item straight into the bottle rather than in the cauldron and if so you might like to first cleanse inside it with smudge or incense.

3. Place each item into your chosen vessel and as you do so ask for the plant spirit to be with you to help with your chosen intention and thank each one.

4. Once everything is in the cauldron, stir it gently with a spoon and really feel the vibration of your intention. If it is calm you want, then calm you need to be. Embody that which you want to manifest, remembering that you must become the vibration of what you want to manifest in order for it to come to you.

5. Transfer the mixture of items to the bottle.

6. You could seal the bottle with a beautiful wax seal or attach dried flowers, herbs or crystals to the bottle and possibly attach a brown craft tag with hessian string. Please always use natural items: with everything you craft you must be mindful of where it might end up, and if you attach glitter or plastic shapes these will one day end up in landfill.

Other options you might like to add include oils or infused oils. If you add plain oil to the mix you might then use the oil as an anointing oil after a month of infusing.

Below are some suggestions you might like to use in your spirit or spell bottle for specific purposes. You can pick whatever you have on hand and use whatever quantities you feel guided to use:

* Abundance: alkanet root, allspice, basil, bergamot (wild), cinnamon, ginger, orange rind, poppy (wild and/or seeds), citrine, green or yellow crystals.

* Calm: chamomile flowers, California poppy, catnip, fennel, lavender, passionflower, tarragon, valerian, brown or black grounding crystals.

* Courage: borage, chaga mushrooms, comfrey, dandelion, dragon's blood resin, licorice root, mullein, oak, St John's wort, sunflower, tarragon or thyme. I like to work with red and yellow crystals for courage because courage is related to the base and solar plexus chakras, so you might also like to include red or yellow dried flowers.

* Cleansing: alkanet root, bay leaf, bergamot (wild), broom, clove, copal resin, eucalyptus, palo santo, sage, white sage, black tourmaline, shungite or selenite.

* Divination and vision: alder, bay leaf, bergamot (wild), birch, cinnamon, dandelion, eyebright, hazel, mugwort, nutmeg, oak, pussy willow, rowan, wormwood, willow or yarrow. Because divination and insight are related to the third eye chakra I use purple or clear/white crystals such as amethyst, clear quartz and white stones.

* Love: apple, basil, birch, cacao, catnip, chamomile, cinnamon, clove, cranberries, dragon's blood resin, ginger, hawthorn, hibiscus, holly, honey, licorice, mistletoe, nutmeg, oak (oak and mistletoe make a very magickal combination), pomegranate, poppy (wild), sweet violet, vanilla, yarrow, ylang ylang, rose quartz, pink or green crystals.

* Protection: alder, bay leaf, blackthorn, bougainvillea, cinnamon, clove, copal, frankincense, garlic, holly, juniper, mugwort, mullein, nettle, oak, oregano, parsley, pepper, pine, rowan, salt, tarragon, thyme, turmeric, white sage, wormwood, yarrow, yellow dock, black stones, onyx, obsidian or black tourmaline crystals.

MEDICINE POUCHES

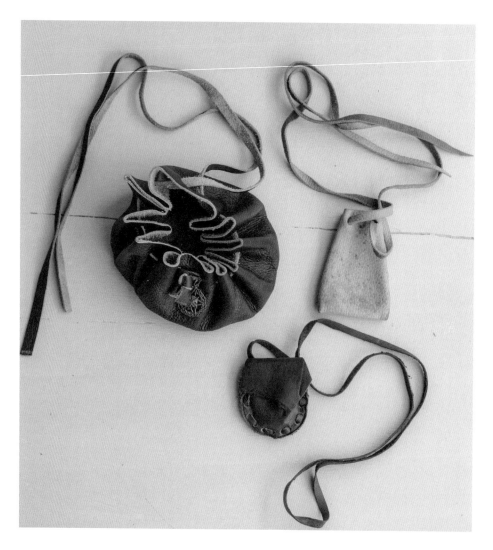

Medicine pouches.

The same items you put inside a spirit bottle can be placed in a medicine pouch. These beautiful creations have been worn for centuries by various cultures to hold their special medicine in. Some people carry items such as tobacco to give as offerings to plants when they pick them, some carry other medicines depending on where they are going while others carry precious items that hold importance to the wearer. Whatever the purpose, I love wearing them close to my heart and knowing that we can carry beautiful spirit medicine with us anywhere we go.

Below are a few suggestions for items to include that would make potent medicine pouches:

* Healing: green is a very healing colour, along with pink and gold. You could place a gold piece of jewellery, rose quartz, pink flowers or green stones in your pouch as well as chickweed, cinnamon, comfrey, elder, frankincense, juniper, lime, marjoram, marshmallow, mint, mullein, myrrh, oregano, pine, plantain, saffron, sage, self-heal, sesame, sweet violet, vanilla or yarrow.

* Luck: this is an interesting topic, for what really is luck? Some people have it, some don't, so is it merely the fact that you are not vibrationally aligned to what you are trying to achieve or is your bad luck a gift for you to learn from? I see lucky talismans as a way of clearing what is really holding me back from achieving my goals, or something that allows me to see the meaning in the cards I am dealt. To attract luck you can try alkanet root, allspice, apple, ash, California poppy, herb Robert, holly, nutmeg, orange, parsley, pomegranate, poppy (wild), pussy willow, saffron or strawberry.

* Peace: borage, bougainvillea, chamomile, meadowsweet, marshmallow, myrrh, sweet violet, tea or yarrow. I find pastel-coloured stones and scolecite good to bring in a sense of peace, while rose quartz, green calcite, selenite, angelite and celestite are also good choices.

* Wisdom: it comes as no surprise to me that most on the list for wisdom are trees or are related to them, because trees hold the wisdom of the ages. They are incredible beings to work with: strong, calm, slow and reliable. To attract wisdom try ash, birch, cedar, eyebright, hazelnut, oak, reishi mushroom, rowan or white sage. For crystals use petrified wood, brown stones, amethyst, purple or white stones.

RITUAL SALTS

Ritual salts are quick and easy to make and can have a myriad of wonderful benefits. We can use them in our ritual practices or place them in spirit bottles, medicine pouches or straight into the bath. We can create salts with many ingredients or stick with one and immerse ourselves in its energy. Salt is known for its cleansing, purification and protective qualities on its own, so adding ingredients to it really binds and amplifies everything together.

Recipe: black ritual salt

Black salt is a well-known salt for banishing and protecting a space. If you feel you need to protect your ritual space, home or room this should be your go-to recipe. You will need equal quantities of each of the following ingredients.

EQUIPMENT/ INGREDIENTS

- mortar and pestle
- glass jar with a lid

* salt
* pepper
* ash and/or charcoal (from your fireplace or ash from burned incense)
* eggshells, optional

DIRECTIONS

I like to grind up the ingredients for this recipe in a mortar and pestle. As you grind the ingredients more and more finely, really instil your intention.

1. Either place each ingredient in a mortar and pestle and grind, or do one at a time and add to a cauldron with your intention.

2. If you are using eggshells, make sure they are dry then grind them as close to a fine powder as possible. You might like to sift it if there are large pieces to remove.

3. Once everything is ground up to the desired consistency, state your intention again while stirring it all together.

4. Put the mixture into the jar and seal. Store until needed.

To use, sprinkle the salt around the perimeter of your ritual area, room or property or wherever you feel you need protection.

Bath salts

I love making up a jar of bath salts and keeping it near the bath in a beautiful amber glass apothecary bottle for when I need it. They make excellent gifts, especially when you have poured your intentions and magick into them.

Method: **basic bath salt recipe**

EQUIPMENT/ INGREDIENTS

- cauldron
- glass jar with airtight lid
- ✱ 1 cup Epsom salts
- ✱ 1 cup pink or sea salt or a combination
- ✱ 2 tbs bicarbonate of soda, optional
- ✱ 1 tsp pink or green clay, optional
- ✱ 2 g/0.07 oz essential oil/s
- ✱ dried flowers or herbs: good choices include lavender, borage, calendula petals, rose petals or elderflower (as much or as little as you like)

DIRECTIONS

1. Place the Epsom salts, pink salt, bicarbonate of soda and clay in the cauldron and stir well to combine.

2. Add the essential oils and thoroughly combine.

3. Add the dried herbs or flowers, mix again and pour into the glass jar.

On the following page are some additions you could add to the basic salt recipe.

Recipe: REFRESH bath salt

Sometimes a bath can completely zap us and usually it's because we are in desperate need of relaxation, or maybe it's the wine … Anyway, sometimes it's nice to take a bath and feel refreshed, for which you might choose essential oils for their uplifting scents such as:

- ✖ basil
- ✖ eucalyptus, including the lemon or peppermint varieties
- ✖ peppermint
- ✖ tea tree

This would look lovely with green clay to complete the earthy experience.

Recipe: FOREST bathing salt

I love anything forest related and forest bathing ritual salts transport me to the forest, where I feel most at home and peaceful. Use any essential oils or a combination of:

- ✖ cedarwood, cypress
- ✖ pine, Scots pine, silver fir
- ✖ vetiver
- ✖ Add a heap of chopped-up pine needles and green clay.

SCRYING

I left scrying until last, because you can do it with many of the creations you can make from this book. Scrying is one of the oldest forms of divination work and can be done with a nice dark cauldron, which makes cast-iron ones perfect for this work although any cauldron or bowl can be used. You can also scry using a mirror, fire, smoke or a reflective surface; black obsidian and onyx are good for this.

'Scrying' is the ability to acquire messages or images from the subconscious and spirit when searching for answers by looking into a reflective surface. We can add aids to the water such as oil, ash or wax, which create their own patterns on the surface and this is where some of your beautiful creations from the book will come into play. Here are some ways you might like to scry:

* ash: add the ash from your incense onto the surface of the water
* brews: tasseography, or tea leaf reading; you can use the leaves from your brews
* candles: drop some wax onto the water
* crystals: crystal balls or obsidian or onyx plates
* fire: watching the flame of a candle or fire or even spirit fire from Chapter 6
* oil: a few drops of oil on water
* smoke: from incense or burning something
* water: using a herbal simmer, brew, water with essences or just water on its own.

Here are some suggestions using particular divination products you might like to try:

* anointing oils made from birch, dandelion, mugwort or yarrow
* essences made from apple, aspen, birch, broom, dandelion, mugwort, pussy willow, rowan, Scots pine, silver fir, willow or yarrow
* incense ash made from mugwort, wormwood or yarrow.

There are many more I could list but these provide a good place to start. Also, hopefully by now the appendices are your best friend.

Method: **SCRYING**

1. Scrying is normally practised at night, when the reflection of the moon can be useful, but can be performed at anytime.

2. It's important to set your space and create your ceremony or ritual.

3. A light trance state is important, as it allows you to see between both states of consciousness. You may like to drum, meditate, light incense or utilise whatever practice you like to gain this space.

4. You may go in search of specific answers to questions or just allow images to come to you. Do not try to decipher them yet; just allow them to come to you and let any ordinary thoughts go.

5. When you have finished you might like to record in your journal what you saw, felt or heard or perhaps draw the images. This process generally allows you to decipher what the messages were as you bring them into the physical.

Final Thoughts

As I write my final thoughts at 11.11 pm I am reminded that spirit is always with me. I thank spirit for being with me as I wrote this book and hope it will inspire you to create and more importantly, gain an amazing connection with the world around you and the world within you.

When we give ourselves the space to *be* in the present and come back to our centre we realise that that is where peace truly lies. Bringing ritual and ceremony into our day is something so simple, yet it has a ripple effect. Start small, make it achievable, make the time and I guarantee you will be rewarded. All our answers lie within. Let the plants guide you and let your soul guide you back home.

Appendix 1

herbal
reference

There are many herbs that I could list here but I want to stick with what is most readily available worldwide. You should always look at what is naturally growing around you, as medicine will show itself where it is needed. You might be surprised by how much you can use that you either already have or can acquire easily. Try to use what is indigenous to your area or culture or grow something you have an affinity with. Start off with one or two herbs and learn them well, then add another when you're ready. Trying to do it all at once can be very overwhelming, so start where you are with what you've got.

I have listed what element, planet and polarity each herb is usually affiliated with. If you are working with feminine, emotional issues you might like to work with the water or yin qualities of a herb, or use another element to help balance out the water such as fire or earth. I label them in terms of yin and yang because these terms mean so much more than just feminine and masculine. For example:

YIN PROPERTIES	YANG PROPERTIES
Feminine, cold, nurturing, creating, soft, slow, flow, descending, hypoactive, dark	Masculine, hot, neglecting, destruction, strong, fast, direct, ascending, hyperactive, light

CAUTIONS

I have also listed the cautions to be aware of when making spiritual preparations, because you are working with medicinal plants that have an effect in the body. The biggest points to keep in mind are:

✖ Anything taken in excess can have adverse effects, so remember that moderation is key.

✖ Never ingest any essential oil, as they are highly concentrated forms of the plant.

✖ There are many species of the same plant, so if you are ingesting or applying anything on your skin please ensure you research your plants thoroughly. If in doubt find a substitute or consider making an essence instead.

✖ Always check what part of the plant is used if you are ingesting it or applying it to your skin.

✖ If you are on any kind of medication such as Warfarin or heart or blood pressure drugs please check with your physician for any interactions.

✖ Although there are many cautions for avoiding certain herbs when pregnant or breastfeeding, essences are considered safe and do not interfere with any medications as they are vibrational.

NAME	ELEMENT/S	PLANET/S OR CELESTIAL BODY	POLARITY	EDIBLE
ALDER (*Alnus glutinosa*)	Water	Venus	Yin	Yes
ALKANET (*Alkanna tinctoria*)	Water	Venus	Yin	No
ALLSPICE (*Pimenta officinalis*)	Fire	Mars	Yang	Yes
APPLE (*Malus sylvestris*)	Water	Venus	Yin	Yes
ASH (*Fraxinus excelsior*)	Fire	Sun	Yang	Yes
ASPEN (*Populus tremula*)	Air	Mercury, Jupiter, Saturn	Yang	Yes
BASIL (*Ocimum basilicum*)	Fire	Mars, Pluto	Yang	Yes
BAY LAUREL (*Laurus nobilis*)	Fire	Sun	Yang	Yes

SPIRITUAL USES	MEDICINAL USES	CAULDRON USES	CAUTIONS
Guidance, breaking new ground, prophecy, warrior, sacrifice, shield, strong connection with water, water resistant, defence, protection, moving forward, strength, endurance	Inner bark or leaves used medicinally, externally for wounds and internally (if dried first) to stop bleeding	Anointing/infused oil, brew, essence, medicine pouch, ritual salt, salve, spirit bottle	
Money, business, luck, remove negativity	Externally for wounds and inflammation	Red dye to colour ointments and candles, incense, infused oil, lotion, salve, spirit bottle	Not to be used internally
Attract money and luck, healing	Digestive aid, anti-inflammatory	Incense, magickal meal, medicine pouch, ritual salt, spirit bottle	
Magick, love, faery connection, healing, immortality, divination, cleansing, purification, energy cleanser, transition between this and the otherworld	Diarrhoea, sore throat, laxative, inflammation externally, liver cleansing, reduces tension, insomnia	Brew, essence, herbal simmer, magickal meal, medicine pouch, potion, spirit bottle	
World tree: used to make spears and magickal staves, direction and application of power, magickal knowledge, strength, endurance, determination, courage	Leaves used for gout and rheumatism, bark for fever and to expel worms; liver and stomach complaints	Brew, essence, medicine pouch, spirit bottle	
Strongly associated with Samhain, connecting with spirit, helpful transition with death (a natural cycle), courage when faced with change, threshold tree, divination, shield, peaceful banishing, moving forward	Fever, nervous complaints	Brew, essence, incense, magickal meal, medicine pouch, spirit bottle	
Wealth, love, banishing	Aromatic, carminative on your digestive system	Herbal simmer, magickal meal, medicine pouch, spirit bottle	
Manifestation, clairvoyance, purification, heighten intuition, ward off negative energy	Aids digestion, relieves stress and anxiety	Brew, essence, herbal simmer, incense, magickal meal, ritual salt, spirit bottle	

NAME	ELEMENT/S	PLANET/S OR CELESTIAL BODY	POLARITY	EDIBLE
BERGAMOT: WILD, ALSO KNOWN AS BEE BALM (*Monarda* spp.)	Air	Mercury, moon	Yin	Yes
BIRCH (*Betula alba, B. pendula*)	Water	Venus, sun	Yin	Yes
BLACKBERRY (*Rubus plicatus, R. villosus*)	Water	Venus	Yin	Yes
BLACKTHORN (*Prunus spinosa*)	Fire	Mars, Saturn	Yang	Berries and flowers only
BOUGAINVILLEA (*Bougainvillea* spp.)	Fire	Pluto, Saturn	Yang	Flowers only
BORAGE (*Borago officinalis*)	Air	Jupiter	Yang	Yes
BROOM (*Cytisus scoparius*)	Air	Mars	Yang	No

SPIRITUAL USES	MEDICINAL USES	CAULDRON USES	CAUTIONS
Letting go, increase psychic powers, attraction (manifestation), soothing	Antibacterial, antifungal, anaesthetic, minor wounds, fever, sleep, stomach concerns	Brew, essence, herbal simmer, infused oil, lotion, magickal meal, potion, ritual bath salt, salve, spirit bottle	Not to be used during pregnancy; not the bergamot used to flavour Earl Grey tea
Beginnings, clarity, light bringer, cleansing, shamanic vision, purifying, renewed vitality, love spells (traditionally made into an oil), fertility, healing, change, moves stagnation, boundaries, connection to the fae	Birch water is highly nutrient dense (usually like maple trees), astringent, good for skin problems, rheumatism, gout and urinary infections	Brew, essence, incense, infused oil, lotion, medicine pouch, salve, spirit bottle	Birch allergy
Community, money, protection, linked with faeries, tenacity, power plant, boundaries, endurance, patience, harvest, timing, connection, binding, abundance, healing	Astringent, toning, diarrhoea, coughs, colds, upset stomachs	Brew, essence, herbal simmer, magickal meal, medicine pouch, potion, spirit bottle	
Cleansing, protection, sacrifice, death, transmutation of your soul, battle, warrior, associated with the goddess the Morrighan and the Cailleach, weapon, endurance, fertility, magickally binding, boundaries, healing trauma	Tonic, colds, cleanser, diarrhoea, kidney and bladder complaints	Dried berries in brews, herbal simmer, essence, medicine pouch, spirit bottle	Seeds and leaves are toxic
Survivor, protection, passion, peace, spiritual connection	Cough remedy, antioxidant	Brew, candles, essence, herbal simmer, infused oil, medicine pouch, ritual salt, spirit bottle	
Courage, for a heavy heart, peace, power	Diuretic, colds, fevers, lung complaints, rheumatism, adrenal tonic, anti-inflammatory, stimulate breast-milk production	Candles, essence, herbal simmer, infused oil, magickal meal, medicine pouch, potion, ritual salt, spirit bottle	Oil should not be used during pregnancy
Cleansing, clear the way, uniting and binding, directness of intent, wielding power, purification, health and well-being, strong visionary capabilities, divination, spirit communication, clarity	Cathartic, diuretic, circulatory disorders, gout, varicose veins	Essence, medicine pouch, spirit bottle	Not to be ingested due to its toxicity

NAME	ELEMENT/S	PLANET/S OR CELESTIAL BODY	POLARITY	EDIBLE
CACAO (*Theobroma cacao*)	Earth, fire	Mars	Yin, yang	Yes
CALENDULA (*Calendula officinalis*)	Fire	Sun	Yang	Yes
CALIFORNIA POPPY (*Eschscholzia californica*)	Fire	Sun	Yang	Yes
CATNIP (*Nepeta cataria*)	Water	Venus	Yin	Yes
CEDARWOOD (*Cedrus* spp.)	Fire	Sun	Yang	Some species only
CHAGA MUSHROOM (*Inonotus obliquus*)	No definitive details available	No definitive details available	Yin	Yes

SPIRITUAL USES	MEDICINAL USES	CAULDRON USES	CAUTIONS
Heart-opening medicine, love, money	Antioxidant, lowers blood pressure, improves blood flow, supports cognition and cardiovascular health, increases endorphins to make you feel good, aphrodisiac	Brew, candles (cacao butter), essence, herbal simmer, infused oil, lotion, magickal meal, melt, potion, salve, spirit bottle	
Warmth, movement, helps move stagnation	Lymphatic cleanser, heals skin issues, anti-inflammatory, digestive inflammation such as ulcers and gallbladder issues, antifungal.	Brew, candles, essence, herbal simmer, infused oil, lotion, magickal meal, medicine pouch, melt, potion, ritual salt, salve, spirit bottle	Asteraceae family allergen; avoid high internal doses during pregnancy
Dreams, sleep, relaxation, regeneration, peace, wealth, health, success	Mild sedative, anodyne	Brew, essence, herbal simmer, medicine pouch, potion, spirit bottle	Avoid ingesting if taking sedative medication; mild allergen; avoid during pregnancy
Happiness, love	Fevers, nervousness, pain, flatulence, restlessness, insomnia	Brew, essence, herbal simmer, medicine pouch, potion, ritual salt, spirit bottle	Avoid during pregnancy
Endurance, eternal life, immortality, strength, wisdom, healing, protection	Antiseptic, antifungal, anti-inflammatory, antispasmodic, diuretic, improves hair growth, acne and eczema, anxiety, insomnia, respiratory conditions	Anointing oil, brew, candles, essence, herbal simmer, incense, infused oil, lotion, medicine pouch, melt, ritual salt, salve, spirit bottle	Avoid the berries during pregnancy
The mushroom of immortality: defence, internal strength	Anti-inflammatory, antiviral, antibacterial, immune enhancing, antitumour	Brew, essence, magickal meal, medicine pouch, spirit bottle	Mushroom allergen; avoid with kidney disease or kidney stones; birch tree allergen

NAME	ELEMENT/S	PLANET/S OR CELESTIAL BODY	POLARITY	EDIBLE
CHAMOMILE: COMMON, ROMAN (*Chamaemelum* spp.)	Water	Neptune, sun	Yin	Yes
CHICKWEED (*Stellaria media*)	Water	Moon	Yin	Yes
CINNAMON (*Cinnamomum* spp.)	Fire	Sun	Yang	Yes
CLOVE (*Syzygium aromaticum*)	Fire	Jupiter	Yang	Yes
COCONUT (*Cocos nucifera*)	Water	Moon	Yin	Yes
COMFREY (*Symphytum officinale*)	Water	Saturn	Yin	No
COPAL (*Bursera* spp.)	Fire	Sun	Yang	No

SPIRITUAL USES	MEDICINAL USES	CAULDRON USES	CAUTIONS
Rest, love, money, peace, stress relief	Helps relax your body, calms your digestive tract, insomnia, headache, nervous excitability, neuralgia	Brew, essence, herbal simmer, lotion, magickal meal, melt, potion, ritual salt, salve, spirit bottle	Asteraceae family allergen; do not take with sedative medication; avoid during pregnancy
Love, healing of internal wounds	Internal and external healing, skin conditions – especially itchy ones, haemorrhoids, ulcers	Essence, infused oil, lotion, magickal meal, potion, spirit bottle	
Increase psychic ability, attract wealth, healing, protection, success, spirituality, love	Colds, cramping, nausea, staunches bleeding	Brew, candles, herbal simmer, incense, magickal meal, medicine pouch, potion, spirit bottle	Can lower blood-sugar levels and increase the effects of diabetes medication
Protection, cleansing, love, money	Analgesic, toothache, antiseptic, rheumatism, infections, arthritis, nausea	Brew, herbal simmer, incense, magickal meal, medicine pouch, potion, spirit bottle	
Moon magick, protection, psychic awareness	Antibacterial, antioxidant, skin nourishing	Brew, candles, infused oil, lotion, magickal meal, melt, salve, spirit bottle	
Healing, strength, grounding, drawing together	Strong wound-healing capabilities (known as knit bone)	Infused oil, lotion, medicine pouch, salve, spirit bottle	Traditionally used internally but now not recommended; if applying externally wounds must be closed and thoroughly clean
Protection, cleansing, purifying, love, meditation, removing energy blocks, creating balance, intuition	Calming, anxiety, insomnia, strengthens your mind, healing	Anointing oil, incense, infused oil, medicine pouch, spirit bottle	

NAME	ELEMENT/S	PLANET/S OR CELESTIAL BODY	POLARITY	EDIBLE
CRANBERRY (*Vaccinium macrocarpon, V. oxycoccos*)	Water	Venus	Yin	Yes
CYPRESS (*Cupressus sempervirens*)	Earth	Saturn	Yin	No
DANDELION (*Taraxacum officinale*)	Air, fire	Jupiter, sun, moon	Yang	Yes
DRAGON BLOOD TREE RESIN (*Daemonorops cinnabari*)	Fire	Mars	Yang	No
ELDER (*Sambucus nigra*)	Water	Venus	Yin	Flowers, berries if cooked or tinctured only
EUCALYPTUS (*Eucalyptus* spp.)	Water	Moon	Yin	Leaves if dried first only
EYEBRIGHT (*Euphrasia officinalis*)	Air	Sun	Yang	Yes

SPIRITUAL USES	MEDICINAL USES	CAULDRON USES	CAUTIONS
Love, protection	Urinary infections, anti-inflammatory, improves immune function, lowers blood pressure	Brew, herbal simmer, magickal meal, medicine pouch, potion, spirit bottle	
Everlasting life, transition between life/death/eternal life, hope, eternity, healing, comfort	Astringent, wounds, spasms, clear respiratory congestion, stress	Anointing oil, candles, essence, incense, lotion, ritual salt, salve	Avoid during pregnancy
Joy, divination, manifestation, messages, helps clear fear and anger, internal strength	Liver (root) and kidney (leaf) cleanser, aids digestion, externally for pain and sore muscles, diuretic, anti-inflammatory	Brew, essence, herbal simmer, infused oil, magickal meal, potion, salve, spirit bottle	Asteraceae family allergen
Banishing, love, sexual energy, protection, strength, cleansing of negativity, courage, healing	Skin ulcers, antimicrobial, anti-inflammatory, wounds	Essence, incense, infused oil, lotion, medicine pouch, salve, spirit bottle	
Closure, banishing, strength, regeneration, endings, healing, protection, sacred to the goddess Hecate and the Cailleach, magickal power and teachings, access to the otherworld, connection to faeries and elders, vision, training, facing shadows, shamanic work	Cleanser, hay fever, wounds, bruises, sprains, common remedy as a syrup or tincture for colds	Brew, essence, herbal simmer, incense, infused oil, magickal meal, medicine pouch, potion, spirit bottle	Ingest only processed berries as raw ones can cause nausea and vomiting
Purifying, cleansing of negative energy, protection	Antioxidant, colds, anti-inflammatory, nasal congestion, asthma, stress, pain relief, dry skin	Brew, candles, herbal simmer, incense, infused oil, lotion, medicine pouch, ritual salt, salve, spirit bottle	Drinking tea and use of the oil on skin is not recommended for children
Opens your eyes to see clearly, clairvoyance, second sight	Inflammatory eye disease, hay fever, catarrh, nasal congestion	Brew, candles, essence, herbal simmer, incense, infused oil, medicine pouch, potion, spirit bottle	Avoid during pregnancy or while breastfeeding

NAME	ELEMENT/S	PLANET/S OR CELESTIAL BODY	POLARITY	EDIBLE
FENNEL (*Foeniculum vulgare*)	Fire	Mercury	Yang	Seeds
FERN, MALE (*Dryopteris filix-mas*)	Air	Mercury	Yang	No
FRANKINCENSE (*Boswellia* spp.)	Fire	Sun	Yang	The translucent resin only
GARLIC (*Allium sativum*)	Fire	Mars	Yang	Yes
GINGER (*Zingiber officinale*)	Fire	Mars	Yang	Yes
GORSE (*Ulex europaeaus*)	Fire	Mars, sun	Yang	Flowers only

SPIRITUAL USES	MEDICINAL USES	CAULDRON USES	CAUTIONS
Calming, purification, healing	Flatulence, griping pain	Brew, herbal simmer, magickal meal, medicine pouch, flavouring, spirit bottle	Will increase the flow of breast milk
Camouflage, invisibility, strong connection to the fae, uncovering secrets and hidden knowledge, protection, luck	Tapeworm, abscesses, boils, nose bleeds, carbuncles, sores, antibacterial, antiviral, anti-inflammatory, anodyne	Essence, medicine pouch, spirit bottle	Some ferns are poisonous
Consecration, protection, healing, love, lifting vibration	Wounds, stress, tension, arthritis, improve gut function, asthma, oral health, anti-inflammatory, reduce signs of ageing, astringent, pain, boosts immune function, improves concentration	Anointing oil, candles, essence, incense, infused oil, magickal meal, medicine pouch, melt, potion, salve, spirit bottle	
Banishing, healing, protection	Antiseptic, natural antibiotic, coughs, colds, asthma	Brew, herbal simmer, magickal meal, medicine pouch, potion, ritual salt, spirit bottle	Do not make a garlic-infused oil for cooking as there is a high chance of botulism
Money, love, cleansing, fire, passion, positive changes, abundance, luck	Increases peripheral blood circulation, promotes perspiration, carminative on your digestive system, externally on muscle sprains	Brew, essence, herbal simmer, incense, magickal meal, medicine pouch, potion, ritual salt, spirit bottle	Avoid high doses during pregnancy
Fertility, vitality, creativity, connected with the god Lugh, warrior, strength, mental agility, desire, arousal, passion, connected with faeries, partnership, love magick, protection, boundaries, vitality, strong association with the solar plexus chakra	Traditionally used for kidney stones, coughs, colds, asthma, swellings, general tonic	Anointing oil, brew, essence, herbal simmer, magickal meal, medicine pouch, potion, salve, spirit bottle	Ingest the flowers only in small amounts

NAME	ELEMENT/S	PLANET/S OR CELESTIAL BODY	POLARITY	EDIBLE
HAWTHORN (*Crataegus* spp.)	Fire	Mars	Yang	Berries and flowers only
HAZEL (*Corylus* spp.)	Water	Mercury	Yin	Nuts only
HEATHER (*Calluna vulgaris*)	Water	Venus	Yin	Flowering tops only
HERB ROBERT (*Geranium robertianum*)	Water	Venus	Yin	Yes
HIBISCUS (*Hibiscus* spp.)	Water	Venus	Yin	Yes
HOLLY (*Ilex aquifolium*)	Fire	Saturn, sun	Yang	Yes
HONEY	Air	Sun	Yin	Yes

SPIRITUAL USES	MEDICINAL USES	CAULDRON USES	CAUTIONS
Cleansing, connected with faeries, associated with Beltane/ May Day, marriages, love	Beneficial for your heart and blood pressure, cardiac tonic, hypotensive, improves blood flow, antioxidant, anti-inflammatory	Brew, essence, herbal simmer, magickal meal, medicine pouch, potion, spirit bottle	Do not use if taking heart or blood-pressure medication or have high or low blood pressure; do not ingest during pregnancy or lactation, should only be used internally through a qualified herbalist
Strong Celtic connection with wisdom, magick, knowledge and an awareness of all, inspiration, awe, love, fertility, highly protective	Powdered and mixed with honey for coughs, nutritious, reduces blood pressure, anti-inflammatory, aids digestion, antioxidant	Essence, magickal meal, medicine pouch, spirit bottle	
Life and death, strong relationship with bees, related to the goddess Brighid, protection, growth, reconnection, love, helping you move forward in flow, good fortune, nurturing	Antiseptic, expectorant, wounds, diuretic, coughs, colds, kidney and bladder conditions, arthritis and rheumatism	Brew, essence, herbal simmer, lotion, magickal meal, medicine pouch, potion, spirit bottle	Can raise blood pressure slightly
Good luck, fertility, strength, gentleness, love, beauty	Sore throats, skin and eye irritations, peptic ulcer, haemorrhages, diarrhoea, leaves for wounds, sedative and astringent	Brew, flower essence, infused oil, lotion, medicine pouch, potion, salve, spirit bottle	
Love, passion, lust	Antioxidant, boosts immune system, anti-inflammatory, lowers blood pressure	Brew, essence, herbal simmer, magickal meal, medicine pouch, potion, spirit bottle	Malvaceae family allergen; use with caution with high or low blood pressure
Protection (especially during winter), luck, endurance, passion, love, sleep magick, warrior spirit	Coughs, colds, gout, arthritis, rheumatism	Brew (weak), essence, incense, medicine pouch, spirit bottle	Do not ingest the berries
Binding, healing, love, prosperity	Anti-inflammatory, antioxidant, antibacterial, burns, wounds, coughs	Brew, lotion, magickal meal, melt, potion, spirit bottle	Can cause reactions in some people

NAME	ELEMENT/S	PLANET/S OR CELESTIAL BODY	POLARITY	EDIBLE
IVY (*Hedera helix*)	Water	Saturn, moon	Yin	No
JASMINE (*Jasminum* spp.)	Water	Moon	Yin	Flowers but only certain varieties
JUNIPER (*Juniperus communis*)	Fire	Saturn, sun	Yang	Berries only
LAVENDER (*Lavandula angustifolia*)	Air	Mercury	Yang	Flowers only
LEMON (*Citrus limon*)	Water	Moon	Yin	Yes
LEMON VERBENA (*Lippia citriodora*)	Air	Mercury	Yang	Leaves only

SPIRITUAL USES	MEDICINAL USES	CAULDRON USES	CAUTIONS
Labyrinth, protection, healing, support, connection, spiral growth, strength, persistence, team work, immortality, strength in community, connection with the goddess Arianrhod and wisdom	Traditionally used for external conditions but no longer recommended because of its toxicity	Essence, medicine pouch, spirit bottle	Highly toxic
Purity, sensuality, inspiration, devotion, love, money	Antioxidant, digestive health, oral health, heart health, depression, anxiety, calms your nervous system, aphrodisiac	Anointing oil, brew, essence, infused oil, lotion, magickal meal, medicine pouch, melt, potion, salve, spirit bottle	Only ingest *Jasminus officinale, J. sambac* and *J. grandiflorum*
Healing, protection	Diuretic, urinary antiseptic, cystitis	The berries that flavour gin, brew, essence, herbal simmer, magickal meal, potion, spirit bottle	Should be avoided during pregnancy and by those with kidney disease
Meditation, relaxing, protection, cleansing	Anxiety, insomnia, burns, wounds, headaches, depression	Brew, candles, essence herbal simmer, incense, infused oil, lotion, magickal meal, medicine pouch, melt, potion, ritual salt, salve, spirit bottle	Essential oil can lower blood pressure and should not be used on open wounds
Moon magick, purification, love	High in vitamin C, antioxidant, improves digestion, immune boosting	Brew, candles, essence, herbal simmer, incense, magickal meals, medicine pouch, melts, potion, spirit bottle	Can aggravate stomach problems and mouth sores; citrus allergy
Purification, amplification, love, helps with nightmares	Digestive issues, anxiety, sleep problems	Brew, candles, herbal simmer, incense, magickal meal, medicine pouch, potion, spirit bottle	Has been known to cause allergic reactions

NAME	ELEMENT/S	PLANET/S OR CELESTIAL BODY	POLARITY	EDIBLE
LICORICE (*Glycyrrhiza glabra*)	Water	Mercury, Venus, Jupiter	Yin	Root only
LIME (*Citrus* spp.)	Fire	Uranus, sun	Yang	Fruit only
LION'S MANE MUSHROOM (*Hericium erinaceus*)	Earth	No definitive details available	Yin	Yes
MAPLE (*Acer* spp.)	Fire, water	Jupiter	Yin, yang	Leaves, bark and syrup only
MARSHMALLOW (*Althaea officinalis*)	Water	Venus, moon	Yin	Yes
MEADOSWEET (*Filipendula ulmaria*)	Air	Jupiter	Yang	Yes
MINT (*Mentha* spp.)	Air	Mercury	Yang	Yes

SPIRITUAL USES	MEDICINAL USES	CAULDRON USES	CAUTIONS
Binds and heightens power, to attract, guides, synergise love, willpower and empowerment	Dry cough, lung complaints, expectorant, soothing, anti-spasmodic, synergises herbs, guides herbs in your body, gastric ulcers, acid reflux	Brew, essence, incense, medicine pouch, spirit bottle	Can raise blood pressure so should not be taken during pregnancy or by those with high blood pressure; not to be taken long term
Love, healing, purification	High in vitamin C, improves immune system, antioxidant, improves digestion, skin health	Brew, candles, essence, herbal simmer, incense, magickal meal, medicine pouch, melt, potion, spirit bottle	Can cause gastrointestinal irritation or accentuate stomach problems or mouth ulcers; avoid with kidney issues; citrus allergy
Calm, restoring, flow, reconnecting to the spirit realm, spiritual growth	Memory, focus, calming and healing for your nervous system, anxiety, anti-inflammatory, improves clarity, concentration, increases energy	Brew, magickal meal, spirit bottle	May cause abdominal discomfort; mushroom allergen
Strength, balance, abundance, love, longevity, money, new beginnings, hope, repel evil, protection	Good for easing pains of your liver and spleen, red maple is astringent, maple syrup is a natural sugar substitute	Brew (syrup), essence, magickal meal (syrup), medicine pouch, potion, spirit bottle	Red maple leaves are toxic
Protection, cleansing, love, death, rebirth, fertility, attraction, soothing, comforting	Soothing agent for internal and external use, inflammation, irritation of your urinary and digestive systems	Brew, essence, incense, infused oil, medicine pouch, potion, salve, spirit bottle	Can slow the absorption of medications
Peace, love, happiness, divination	Rheumatism, antiseptic, astringent, dyspepsia, diuretic, heartburn, peptic ulcer	Brew, essence, medicine pouch, potion, spirit bottle	Salicylate sensitivity; avoid with antiplatelet/ anticoagulant/ NSAIDs medications or aspirin allergy
Purification, healing, money	Flatulence, anti-spasmodic, stimulant	Brew, essence, herbal simmer, magickal meal, potion, spirit bottle	Lamiaceae family allergen

NAME	ELEMENT/S	PLANET/S OR CELESTIAL BODY	POLARITY	EDIBLE
MISTLETOE (*Viscum album*)	Air	Jupiter, sun	Yang	No
MOTHERWORT (*Leonurus cardiaca*)	Earth	Venus	Yin	Yes
MUGWORT (*Artemisia vulgaris*)	Earth	Venus, moon	Yes	Yes
MULLEIN (*Verbascum thapsus*)	Fire	Saturn	Yin, yang	Yes
MYRRH (*Commiphora myrrha*)	Water	Moon	Yin	Rarely
NETTLE (*Urtica dioica*)	Fire	Mars	Yang	Yes
NUTMEG (*Myristica fragrans*)	Air, fire	Mercury, Jupiter	Yang	Yes, in small amounts

SPIRITUAL USES	MEDICINAL USES	CAULDRON USES	CAUTIONS
Romance, love, fertility, strength, courage, protects the wearer from negativity	Nerve tonic, epilepsy, wounds, used by druids and shamans as an hallucinogenic	Essence, medicine pouch, spirit bottle	Do not ingest the berries due to their toxicity
Courage, strength, joy, strengthens and calms your heart centre and a restless spirit	Heart and digestive and female reproductive issues, anxiety, sedative	Brew, essence, herbal simmer, potion, spirit bottle	Not to be used during pregnancy or by people on heart medication; Lamiaceae family allergen
For visionary and divination work, strong protection from negative influences and nightmares, lucid dreaming, boundaries, expelling, protection, creativity, inspiration, encourages flow, expansion	Poor menstrual flow, digestive stimulant, depression, tension	Anointing oil, brew, herbal simmer, incense, infused oil, medicine pouch, salve, spirit bottle	Caution must be exercised when ingesting as mugwort can stimulate your uterus and menstruation; do not drink during pregnancy; should be avoided if you have heavy menstrual flows
Healing, protection, standing tall, strength, self-reliance, focus, grounding, uplifting, positivity, courage, higher perspective, shining your light	Lung conditions, pain relief, sedative, ear troubles, externally for inflammation	Brew, candles, essence, herbal simmer, infused oil, lotion, medicine pouch, potion, salve, spirit bottle	Do not use mullein oil in your ear if it is ruptured
Healing, protection, consecration, peace, cleansing	Wounds, infections, ulcers, antimicrobial, anti-inflammatory, spasms, oral ulcers	Anointing oil, candles, essence, incense, infused oil, lotion, medicine pouch, melt, salve, spirit bottle	Avoid during pregnancy
Protection, banishing, fertility, threshold guardian, nourishing, boundaries, doorway between life and death	Nutritive, diuretic, cystitis, anaemia, blood tonic, cleansing, childhood eczema, haemorrhage	Brew, essence, infused oil, medicine pouch, potion, salve, spirit bottle	Use caution when handling fresh plants as they cause quite a sting
Increases psychic abilities and spiritual connection, banishing, reveals truth, love, luck, money, confidence	Antioxidant, anti-inflammatory, relieves pain, soothes digestion, antibacterial	Brew, candles, essence, herbal simmer, incense, magickal meal, medicine pouch, potion, ritual salt, spirit bottle	Always use sparingly if ingesting

NAME	ELEMENT/S	PLANET/S OR CELESTIAL BODY	POLARITY	EDIBLE
OAK (*Quercus* spp.)	Fire	Jupiter, sun	Yang	Yes
OAT (*Avena sativa*)	Earth	Venus	Yin	Yes
ONION (*Allium cepa*)	Fire	Mars	Yang	Yes
ORANGE (*Citrus sinensis*)	Fire	Sun	Yang	Fruit only
OREGANO (*Origanum vulgare*)	Air	Mercury	Yang	Yes
PALO SANTO (*Bursera graveolens*)	Air, water	Venus, Mercury	Yin, yang	Yes
PAPRIKA (TRADITIONALLY FROM *Capsicum annuum*)	Fire	Mars	Yang	Yes
PARSLEY (*Petroselinum crispum*)	Air	Mercury	Yang	Yes

SPIRITUAL USES	MEDICINAL USES	CAULDRON USES	CAUTIONS
Access to other realms, balance, strength, courage, endurance, protection, love, fertility, luck, wealth, sustaining growth over time, magickally connected with mistletoe to increase power	Antiseptic, anti-inflammatory making it good for wounds, astringent, diarrhoea, haemorrhage, fever, sore throat, phlegm, varicose veins, burns, prolapse	Anointing oil, brew, essence, infused oil, lotion, magickal meal (acorn flour), medicine pouch, potion, salve, spirit bottle	If using internally the bark should be taken from branches in early spring
Money, support, strength, prosperity	Nervine tonic, exhaustion, externally soothing for skin	Essence, magickal meal, melt, spirit bottle	Can cause gas and bloating; oat allergies are known
Rebirth, regeneration, protection	Coughs, phlegm, antiseptic, diuretic	Magickal meal, ritual salt, spirit bottle	Onion allergies are known
Love, luck, wealth	Aids iron absorption, improves digestion, supports immune system, anti-inflammatory, antimicrobial, antioxidant	Brew, candles, herbal simmer, incense, magickal meal, medicine pouch, melt, potion, ritual salt, spirit bottle	Citrus allergy; may potentiate heartburn
Protection, healing, money	Antiviral, improves immunity and digestion, antibacterial, anti-inflammatory	Brew, herbal simmer, infused oil, magickal meal, medicine pouch, potion, ritual salt, spirit bottle	Lamiaceae family allergen
Cleansing, grounding, sacred, transformation, purification, serenity, tranquillity, inspires creativity, love, good fortune, deep connection to source, raises vibration, expels negative energy	Lung conditions, anxiety, stress, uplifts mood, pain, headaches, allergies, immune boosting	Candles, essence, herbal simmer, incense, infused oil, lotion, medicine pouch, melt, potion, salve, spirit bottle	Avoid during pregnancy
Creativity, enhancer	Anti-inflammatory, arthritis, aids digestion, acne, burns, antimicrobial, high vitamin content, wound healing, increases blood circulation	Incense, magickal meal, medicine pouch, spirit bottle	Mildly spicy so care should be taken with dosage; paprika allergy
Purification, honouring the dead, communication with spirit, luck, fertility, banishes negative energies, protection, love	Comforts your stomach, promotes urine production, diuretic	Herbal simmer, magickal meal, medicine pouch, potion, ritual salt, spirit bottle	Do not use medicinal dosages during pregnancy as they can stimulate the womb

NAME	ELEMENT/S	PLANET/S OR CELESTIAL BODY	POLARITY	EDIBLE
PASSIONFLOWER (*Passiflora incarnata*)	Water	Venus	Yin	Yes
PATCHOULI (*Pogostemon* spp.)	Earth	Saturn	Yin	Leaves only; the essential oil form is not edible
PEPPER, BLACK (*Piper nigrum*)	Fire	Mars	Yang	Yes
PEPPERMINT (*Mentha piperita*)	Air, fire	Venus, Mercury	Yang	Yes
PINE (*Pinus* spp.)	Air	Mars	Yang	Needles only
PLANTAIN (*Plantago major*)	Earth	Venus	Yin	Yes
POMEGRANATE (*Punica granatum*)	Fire	Mercury	Yang	Yes
POPPY, WILD (*Papaver rhoeas*)	Water	Moon	Yin	Petals only

SPIRITUAL USES	MEDICINAL USES	CAULDRON USES	CAUTIONS
Passion, relaxation, spirit connection, insight	Sedative, calming, anxiety, insomnia, nerve pain, shingles	Brew, essence, herbal simmer, medicine pouch, potion, ritual salt, spirit bottle	Avoid if taking sedative medication or during pregnancy
The oil of peace: brings a sense of clarity, prosperity, fertility, love	Skin conditions, antiseptic, diuretic, constipation, bowel problems	Essence, incense, magickal meal, medicine pouch, melt, ritual salt, spirit bottle; the *leaves* for a brew or herbal simmer; the *oil* for candles, melts, salts	Do not ingest the essential oil
Banishing, protection	Antioxidant, anti-inflammatory, aids digestion, antimicrobial	Magickal meal, medicine pouch, ritual salt, spirit bottle	Pepper allergy
Love, psychic enhancement, spiritual growth, dispel negative energy	Nausea, flatulence, vomiting, intestinal colic, ulcerative colitis, Crohn's disease	Brew, candles, herbal simmer, incense, infused oil, magickal meal, medicine pouch, melt, potion, ritual salt, spirit bottle	Lamiaceae family allergen
Protection, healing, fertility, money	Chest infections, colds, circulation problems, rheumatism, muscular aches and pains	*Needles* for brew, essence, herbal simmer/incense, salt; *resin* for infused oil, salve, medicine pouch, spirit bottle; *essential oil* for candles, herbal simmer, melt, salt	Pine allergy; avoid during pregnancy
Internal healing on a metaphysical level, drawing out what does not serve you, strength, protection	Wound healing and drawing out, anti-inflammatory, expectorant, soothes inflamed membranes, astringent	Brew, herbal simmer, infused oil, lotion, magickal meal, medicine pouch, potion, ritual salt, salve, spirit bottle	Can cause hay fever
Longevity, fertility, love, luck, protection	Antioxidant, heart, urinary and brain health, immunity, nutrient dense, anti-inflammatory	Herbal simmer, magickal meal, medicine pouch, potion, spirit bottle	Pomegranate allergy
Remembrance, sleep, death, regeneration, undying love (red), success, good fortune, fertility, abundance	Coughs, mild sedative	Brew, essence, herbal simmer, medicine pouch, potion, ritual salt, spirit bottle, add colour to tea	

NAME	ELEMENT/S	PLANET/S OR CELESTIAL BODY	POLARITY	EDIBLE
POPPY SEED (*Papaver somniferum*)	Water	Moon	Yin	Yes
PUSSY WILLOW (*Salix caprea*); *see also* WILLOW	Water	Moon	Yin	Yes
RASPBERRY (*Rubus idaeus*)	Water	Venus	Yin	Yes
REED (*Phragmites australis*)	Water	Moon	Yin	Yes
REISHI MUSHROOM (*Ganoderma lucidum*)	No definitive details available	Jupiter, sun	Yang	Yes
ROSE (*Rosa* spp.)	Water	Venus	Yin	Petals only if organic
ROSEMARY (*Rosmarinus officinalis*)	Fire	Sun	Yang	Yes

SPIRITUAL USES	MEDICINAL USES	CAULDRON USES	CAUTIONS
Moon magick, money, love, fertility	Good source of fibre, nutrient dense	Brew, magickal meal, medicine pouch, ritual salt, spirit bottle	Poppy seed allergy; avoid the tea during pregnancy; seeds from shops are cleaned of any opium before sale
Flow, flexibility, emotions, related to Cerridwen, seership, clairvoyance, empathy, standing between two worlds, shamanic journeying, divine inspiration, connection with bees and honey, comforter, healer of sorrow, letting go	Pain relieving, stops bleeding, gargle for sore throats and wounds	Essence, herbal simmer, medicine pouch, spirit bottle	Common allergen
Protection, love, fertility, attraction, passion	*Leaves* tone your uterus, anti-inflammatory, morning sickness, digestive support; *berries* are nutrient dense, antioxidant	Brew, essence, herbal simmer, magickal meal, medicine pouch, potion, spirit bottle	1 cup only of raspberry leaf tea during pregnancy over 32 weeks; raspberry allergy
Direction, associated with the goddess Brighid, help aim, healing	Bronchitis, stops bleeding and vomiting, lowers fevers, diarrhoea	Essence, medicine pouch, spirit bottle	Reed allergy
The spirit herb: bridges heaven and earth, calms the heart and spirit.	Enhances immune system, improves sleep, antioxidant, helps your body adapt to stress, supports the liver	Brew, essence, herbal simmer, magickal meal, medicine pouch, potion, spirit bottle	Mushroom allergy
The flower of love: depending on the colour can signify different types of emotions, psychic power, healing, luck, protection	Balance hormones, inflammation, coughs, restful sleep, soothes emotions, antioxidant	Anointing oil, brew, candles, essence, herbal simmer, incense, infused oil, lotion, magickal meal, medicine pouch, melt, potion, ritual salt, salve, spirit bottle	Rose allergy
The memory herb: cleansing, protection including psychic, love, healing	Headache, gastric disturbance, boosts immune and circulatory systems, scalp tonic, nervine, tension, depression	Brew, candles, essence, herbal simmer, incense, infused oil, lotion, magickal meal, medicine pouch, melt, potion, ritual salt, salve, spirit bottle	Lamiaceae family allergen; not to be used in medical doses during pregnancy

NAME	ELEMENT/S	PLANET/S OR CELESTIAL BODY	POLARITY	EDIBLE
ROWAN (*Sorbus aucuparia*)	Fire	Sun	Yang	Berries only
SAFFRON, WILD (*Carthamus tinctorius*)	Fire	Sun	Yang	Yes
SAGE (*Salvia officinalis*)	Air	Jupiter	Yang	Yes
SALT	Earth, water	Earth	Neutral, yin	Yes
SANDALWOOD (*Santalum* spp.)	Water	Pluto, moon	Yin	Nuts only
SCOTS PINE (*Pinus sylvestris*)	Air	Mars	Yang	No (available as an essential oil)
SELF-HEAL (*Prunella vulgaris*)	No definitive details available	Venus	Yin	Yes

SPIRITUAL USES	MEDICINAL USES	CAULDRON USES	CAUTIONS
Powerful protector, divine knowledge, magickal, insight, prophecy, vision, passion, connection with Celtic deities Brighid, Cernunnos, Herne and the Dagdha	High in vitamin C so good for your immune system, astringent, diuretic, anti-inflammatory	Essence, herbal simmer, magickal meal, medicine pouch, potion, spirit bottle	Raw berries are poisonous to children; rowan tree allergy
Strength, luck, healing, love	Antioxidant, may improve mood and reduce PMS, aphrodisiac	Herbal simmer, magickal meal, medicine pouch, melt, potion, spirit bottle	Saffron allergy
Healing, cleansing, dispels negativity, protection, wisdom	Sore throats, memory, menopausal hot flushes, skin healing, cold sores	Brew, essence, herbal simmer, incense, infused oil, lotion, magickal meal, medicine pouch, potion, ritual salt, salve, spirit bottle	Lamiaceae family allergen; okay to use in cooking but not the concentrated form during pregnancy
Cleansing, purification, protection, blessing	Healing, anti-inflammatory, maintains blood pressure, keeps you hydrated, balances electrolytes	Magickal meal, medicine pouch, melt, ritual salt, spirit bottle	Do not use in excess, especially if you have high blood pressure
Spiritually healing and uplifting, protection	Acne, menstrual problems, depression, skin infections, sedative	Anointing oil, candles, incense, infused oil, lotion, medicine pouch, melt, ritual salt, salve, spirit bottle	
Vitality, continuity, cleansing, purifying, shamanic visionary work, regeneration, resurrection, access to the upper realms (Gwynfyd, the white life), mental clarity, ideas, decongests	Colds, chest conditions, disinfectant, rheumatism and arthritis, fatigue, sleeplessness, skin cuts and irritations, respiratory antiseptic, decongestant	Herbal simmer, melt, ritual salt, salve, spirit bottle	Avoid the essential oil during pregnancy, for children under 12, if suffering kidney disease or epilepsy and undiluted on your skin
Strength to heal inside and out, spiritual connection (purple flowers)	Healing of internal and external wounds, soothes hot conditions such as sore throats, bronchitis and chest infections, astringent, anti-inflammatory, painkiller, lymphatic, antiviral, allergies	Brew, essence, herbal simmer, infused oil, lotion, medicine pouch, potion, salve, spirit bottle	Lamiaceae family allergen

NAME	ELEMENT/S	PLANET/S OR CELESTIAL BODY	POLARITY	EDIBLE
SILVER FIR (*Abies alba*)	Air	Jupiter, moon	Yin	Yes
STAR ANISE (*Illicium verum*)	Air	Jupiter	Yang	Yes
ST JOHN'S WORT (*Hypericum perforatum*)	Fire	Sun	Yang	Flowers only
STRAWBERRY, WILD (*Fragaria vesca*)	Water	Venus	Yin	Yes
SUNFLOWER (*Helianthus annuus*)	Air	Mercury, sun	Yang	Yes
SWEET VIOLET (*Viola odorata*)	Water	Venus	Yin	Yes
TARRAGON (*Artemisia dracunculus*)	Air	Venus	Yin	Yes

SPIRITUAL USES	MEDICINAL USES	CAULDRON USES	CAUTIONS
Shamanic visionary work, regeneration, resurrection, access to the upper realms (Gwynfyd, the white life), mental clarity, ideas, immortality	Antibiotic, antiseptic, astringent, soothes muscle, helps your respiratory system	Brew, candles, essence, herbal simmer, incense, infused oil, lotion, medicine pouch, melt, ritual salt, salve, spirit bottle	Avoid the essential oil during pregnancy, for children under seven or when suffering kidney disease or epilepsy
Cord cutting, protection, love, increases psychic powers, luck	Respiratory tract infections, nausea, digestive issues, antibacterial, antioxidant, anti-inflammatory, antiviral, antifungal	Candles, essence, herbal simmer, incense, magickal meal, medicine pouch, potion, spirit bottle	Care should be taken to use Chinese star anise and not Japanese, which is highly toxic; do not give to children
Herb of the light, joy, finding your centre or inner light, protection	Nervous system trophorestorative, pain, hormonal issues, nerve damage, insomnia, depression, shingles, wounds, ulcers, burns, swellings	Essence, infused oil (using fresh flowers placed in direct sunlight), medicine pouch, spirit bottle	Many interactions with prescription drugs, including the contraceptive pill; if applied externally can cause photosensitivity
Love, fertility, luck	Antioxidant, improved heart health, anti-inflammatory	Brew, herbal simmer, magickal meal, medicine pouch, potion, spirit bottle	Strawberry allergy
Inner strength, joy, optimism, fertility	Anti-inflammatory, lowers blood pressure, high in nutrients	Brew, essence, herbal simmer, magickal meal, medicine pouch, potion, ritual salt, spirit bottle	Sunflower allergy
Soothes an emotional heart, spiritual uplifting, joy, love, peace, serenity, heart healing, protection, luck	Coughs, antiseptic, flowers are expectorant, eczema, rheumatism, urinary infections, positive effects on your heart, analgesic, arthritis, wounds	Brew, essence, herbal simmer, infused oil, lotion, magickal meal, medicine pouch, potion, ritual salt, salve spirit bottle	Salicylate sensitivity
Calming, protective, compassion, strength and independence after abuse, banishing, bravery, confidence, personal growth	Stimulates appetite, flatulence, digestive issues, promotes menstruation and sleep, anti-inflammatory, pain, indigestion	Brew, herbal simmer, magickal meal, medicine pouch, potion, ritual salt, spirit bottle	Asteraceae family allergen; avoid during pregnancy

NAME	ELEMENT/S	PLANET/S OR CELESTIAL BODY	POLARITY	EDIBLE
TEA (*Camellia sinensis*)	Fire	Mars, sun	Green and white are yin; black is yang	Yes
THYME (*Thymus vulgaris*)	Water	Venus	Yin	Yes
TURKEY TAIL MUSHROOM (*Coriolus versicolor*)	Earth	Venus	Yang	Yes
TURMERIC (*Curcuma longa*)	Water	Mercury, moon	Yin	Yes
VALERIAN (*Valeriana officinalis*)	Water	Venus	Yin	Yes
VANILLA (*Vanilla* spp.)	Water	Venus	Yin	Seed pods only
VERVAIN (*Verbena officinalis*)	Earth	Venus	Yin	Yes

SPIRITUAL USES	MEDICINAL USES	CAULDRON USES	CAUTIONS
Being present, spiritual connection, brings people together, warming, riches, courage, strength	Astringent, diarrhoea, diuretic, antioxidant, benefits the heart, reduces cholesterol, lowers blood pressure, improves focus	Brew, essence, herbal simmer, incense, magickal meal, medicine pouch, potion, spirit bottle	Not recommended for those with constipation or salicylate sensitivity; tannin allergy
Protection, courage, strength, manifestation, purification, sleep, healing, magickal, love	Gastrointestinal disturbances, coughs, sluggish digestion, strong antiseptic, infected wounds, respiratory and digestive infections, sore throats, coughs	Brew, candles, herbal simmer, incense, magickal meal, medicine pouch, potion, ritual salt, spirit bottle	Lamiaceae family allergen; do not use thyme oil internally; avoid medicinal dosages during pregnancy
Spiritual attunement, health and longevity, removes blockages	Adaptogen (helps body adapt to stress), supports immune system and gut health, colds, allergies, anti-cancer properties, anti-inflammatory, antiviral, antibacterial, good for heart and gut health, anxiety	Brew, essence, herbal simmer, magickal meal, potion, spirit bottle	Mushroom allergy
Moon magick, protection, purification	Anti-inflammatory, pain, arthritis, antioxidant, heart health, depression	Brew, magickal meal, medicine pouch, spirit bottle	Not to be used with anticoagulant medication; avoid medicinal dosages during pregnancy; can cause allergy and contact dermatitis in some people
Rest, calm, purification, love, protection	Nervine, tranquillising, neuralgia, tension, anxiety, insomnia, cramps, intestinal colic	Brew, essence, medicine pouch, potion, spirit bottle	Do not take with sedative medication; avoid during pregnancy
Love, self-empowerment, calming, sensuality, seduction, romance, healing, raising vibration, friendship	Aphrodisiac, antioxidant, anti-inflammatory, calming, eases toothache, anxiety	Brew, herbal simmer, infused oil, magickal meal, medicine pouch, melt, potion, salve, spirit bottle	Vanilla allergy
The herb of love and remover of obstacles: purification, peace, healing, sleep, protection, prosperity, related to Cerridwen	Nervine, sedative, astringent, PMT, menopause, tension, depression	Brew, essence, herbal simmer, infused oil, medicine pouch, melt, potion, salve, spirit bottle	Care in people with kidney disease; avoid during pregnancy

NAME	ELEMENT/S	PLANET/S OR CELESTIAL BODY	POLARITY	EDIBLE
VETIVER (*Vetiveria zizanioides*)	Earth	Venus	Yin	Yes, although the essential oil form should not be ingested
WHITE SAGE (*Salvia apiana*)	Air, earth	Jupiter	Yang	Yes
WILLOW (*Salix alba*); *see also* PUSSY WILLOW	Water	Moon	Yin	Bark only
WINE, RED	Earth, fire	Sun	Yang	Yes
WINE, WHITE	Earth, water	Moon	Yin	Yes
WORMWOOD (*Artemisia absinthium*)	Fire	Mars	Yang	Yes, in small quantities only
YARROW (*Achillea millefolium*)	Water	Venus	Yin	Yes
YELLOW DOCK (*Rumex crispus*)	Air	Jupiter	Yang	Roots only

SPIRITUAL USES	MEDICINAL USES	CAULDRON USES	CAUTIONS
The oil of tranquillity: bridges the gap between the spiritual and physical, grounding, calming, money	Nervousness, insomnia, muscle relaxant	Brew, incense, medicine pouch, melt, ritual salt, salve, spirit bottle	Avoid the essential oil during pregnancy
Cleansing, protection, holds wisdom and clarity, balance between body and mind, shamanic journeying	Promotes digestion, clears respiratory tract, fevers, antiseptic, antibacterial, carminative, tonic, heavy menstruation	Anointing oil, candles, essence, herbal simmer, incense, infused oil, medicine pouch, melt, ritual salt, salve, spirit bottle	Avoid ingesting during pregnancy or while breastfeeding; sage allergy
Emotions, divination	Analgesic (where aspirin was initially derived from), anti-inflammatory, antirheumatic, antiseptic, astringent	Brew, essence, herbal simmer, medicine pouch, potion, spirit bottle	Aspirin and salicylate sensitivity; many drug interactions; peptic ulcers; kidney or liver disease; asthma; avoid during pregnancy
Celebration, insightfulness, harvest, love, peace	Antioxidant, expels cold, yang tonic, harmonises blood and qi, can increase the effectiveness of herbal remedies	Essence, potion, spirit bottle	Always drink in moderation
Celebration, purity	Antioxidant, cooling	Essence, potion, spirit bottle	Always drink in moderation
Divination, expulsion, increases psychic abilities, banishing, calling in spirit, clairvoyance, strong protector, attracting love	Expels worms, anti-parasitic	Essence, incense, medicine pouch, ritual salt, spirit bottle	Avoid during pregnancy
Boundaries, increases psychic abilities, protection, dream divination, courage, love, cleansing, healing, balance, peace, positive energy, calmness, sacred in many cultures, wounded warrior	Wounds, astringent, fevers, lowers blood pressure, cystitis, stimulates digestion, tones vessels	Brew, candles, essence, herbal simmer, incense, infused oil, lotion, medicine pouch, melt, potion, ritual salt, salve, spirit bottle	Avoid during pregnancy
The herb of understanding: cord cutting, clears blockages, healing, fertility, money	Chronic skin complaints such as psoriasis, detoxifier, laxative	Brew, essence, potion, ritual salt, spirit bottle	Avoid during pregnancy, when breastfeeding or if you have diarrhoea

NAME	ELEMENT/S	PLANET/S OR CELESTIAL BODY	POLARITY	EDIBLE
YEW (*Taxus baccata*)	Water	Saturn	Yin	No
YLANG YLANG (*Cananga odorata*)	Water	Venus	Yin	Leaves only

SPIRITUAL USES	MEDICINAL USES	CAULDRON USES	CAUTIONS
Associated with Samhain, connection with spirit, endings, beginnings, death and rebirth, knowledge from cycles, ancient wisdom, ancestors, connection with the underworld, protection, preparation for death, infinity	No medicinal uses due to its toxicity	Essence only by placing your bowl of water near the tree	Poisonous: do not ingest and wash your hands after contact
Harmonises masculine and feminine energies, love, attraction, strongly associated with your heart centre, spiritual awakening, joy	Depression, anxiety, high blood pressure, sedative, aphrodisiac	Brew, candles, essence, herbal simmer, incense, infused oil, magickal meal, medicine pouch, melt, potion, ritual salt, salve, spirit bottle	Ylang ylang allergy; the essential oil form should not be ingested

Appendix II

Crystal Reference

I like to keep my crystal selection a simple procedure: I select the crystal that corresponds to the chakra in question. Below is a summary of the seven chakras and their corresponding crystals by colour.

CHAKRA	COLOUR	ELEMENT
BASE	Red	EARTH: your base chakra is associated with your connection to the earth, family, physical energy, survival, courage, stability, material issues, passion and grounding.
SACRAL	Orange	WATER: being of the water element, your sacral chakra is connected with emotions and flow. It is also to do with relationships, desire and pleasure. This chakra is connected with female reproductive organs, which create life and which is why we also associate this chakra with creativity.
SOLAR PLEXUS	Yellow	FIRE: your solar plexus chakra has many functions and is related to your ego, self-esteem, intelligence and assimilation. When you think of fire you can be warmed and comforted or fearful; it has the ability to do both. This chakra is linked to your digestive organs, so how you digest and assimilate are key.

CHAKRA	COLOUR	ELEMENT
HEART	Green, pink	AIR: without air, fire cannot burn. Your solar plexus chakra relies on your heart chakra, as well as your physical body. Your heart chakra is associated with your lungs, which draw in air, and your heart, which draws in blood – thus, it relates to how you draw in life and create balance between your internal and external environments. This is the chakra of love and the connection to your external environment.
THROAT	Blue	ETHER when you look at the elements of each chakra you will notice that your base chakra starts with the heavy earth element, then works up to the fluid but still dense water to fire, which becomes lighter, to air, which is no longer a solid, and up to ether. As you progress upwards this shows how the energy shifts on the scale from grounded, dense earth to the light element of ether. Your throat chakra is the centre for your expression and communication.
THIRD EYE	Purple, indigo	LIGHT: your third eye chakra is well named, as it is all about seeing what can't be seen. You can't see the third eye in the middle of your forehead, but this chakra allows you to sense and see in your mind's eye that which can't be seen by your physical eyes. Personally, I view the third eye chakra as being purple, but you will often see it represented as indigo. Don't get caught up too much on this; just go with whatever sits right with you. If you remember the key lessons of the chakra that is all that matters: the third eye chakra is about 'in-sight' and connection with your spirit guides.
CROWN	White, violet	THOUGHT: your crown chakra may be represented as either white or violet. This chakra is your connection with the universe, just as your base chakra is your connection with the earth. This is where you feel a bond with a higher power, which gives you faith in life, spiritual purpose, wisdom, peace and oneness.

CRYSTAL SUGGESTIONS BY COLOUR

* **Red, base chakra:** red jasper, garnet, red tiger's eye, mookaite, dragon stone, ruby, red agate.

* **Orange, sacral chakra:** citrine (heat treated), stilbite, orange kyanite, sputnik aragonite, copper, tangerine quartz, peach moonstone, sunstone, carnelian, orange calcite.

* **Yellow, solar plexus chakra:** yellow quartz, Libyan tektite, sulphur quartz, chalcopyrite, pyrite, hiddenite, honey calcite, citrine, orange calcite.

* **Green or pink, heart chakra:**

  * **Green:** seraphinite, amazonite, fuchsite, prehnite, green calcite, chrysoprase, grossularite, malachite, peridot, jade, serpentine, epidote, green kyanite, green tourmaline.

  * **Pink:** pink agate, clinoziosite, pink chalcedony, rhodocrosite, mangano calcite, pink petrified wood, rose quartz, pink kunzite, pink tourmaline, cobalto calcite.

* **Blue, throat chakra:** azurite, lapis lazuli, shattuckite, blue kyanite, apatite, K2, angelite, hemimorphite, aragonite, blue fluorite, dumortierite, iolite, blue tiger's eye, covellite, aquamarine, aqua aura quartz, indicolite (blue tourmaline).

* **Purple or indigo, third eye chakra:** amethyst, purple fluorite, lepidolite, charoite, stichtite.

* **Brown:** chiastolite, shaman stone, smoky quartz, dravite, amulet stone, petrified wood, ammonite, coffee moonstone, septarian nodule. Brown stones come in earthen colours and help you ground to the earth. They are wonderful when all your energy is in your head or you are feeling a bit spaced out, and are also great when meditating,

- **Black stones:** black tourmaline, apache tears, hematite, onyx, obsidian, black calcite. The colour black is actually all of the colours of the spectrum, and black stones absorb the colours and also energy. They are very protective stones that will absorb negative energy and are also very grounding stones.

- **Multicoloured stones:** look at what colours are in them and match them up with their respective chakra. Multicoloured stones may aid in linking those colour chakras together or working on both of them at once.

Appendix III

Ogham tree alphabet

The Ogham tree alphabet is a set of symbols that correspond to specific trees and also forms an alphabet that can be used for divination and spiritual growth. When creating things such as essences, candles, spell bottles or medicine pouches you might like to use the symbol to call in the spirit of the tree if you don't physically have it. You could inscribe it into your candle or anoint an object by marking it with the symbol using an anointing oil you have already created. You could also make a set of your own Ogham using sticks, clay and so on.

1. Birch – Beith
2. Rowan – Luis
3. Alder – Fearn
4. Willow – Saille
5. Ash – Nuin
6. Hawthorn – Huath
7. Oak – Duir
8. Holly – Tinne
9. Hazel – Coll
10. Apple – Quert
11. Blackberry/vine – Muin
12. Ivy – Gort
13. Reed – Ngetal
14. Blackthorn – Straif
15. Elder – Ruis
16. Silver fir – Ailim
17. Gorse – Ohn
18. Heather – Ur
19. Poplar/aspen – Eadha
20. Yew – Ioho
21. The grove – The Koad
22. Spindle – Oir
23. Honeysuckle – Uilleand
24. Beech – Phagos
25. The sea – Mor

#	symbol	letters
25		AE, X, XI
24		IO, PH
23		UI, PE, P
22		OI, TH
21		EA, CH, KH
20		I, J, Y
19		E
18		U, W
17		O
16		A
15		R
14		Z, SS, ST
13		P
12		G
11		M
10		Q
9		C, K
8		T
7		D
6		H
5		S
4		F, V, GW
3		N
2		L
1		B

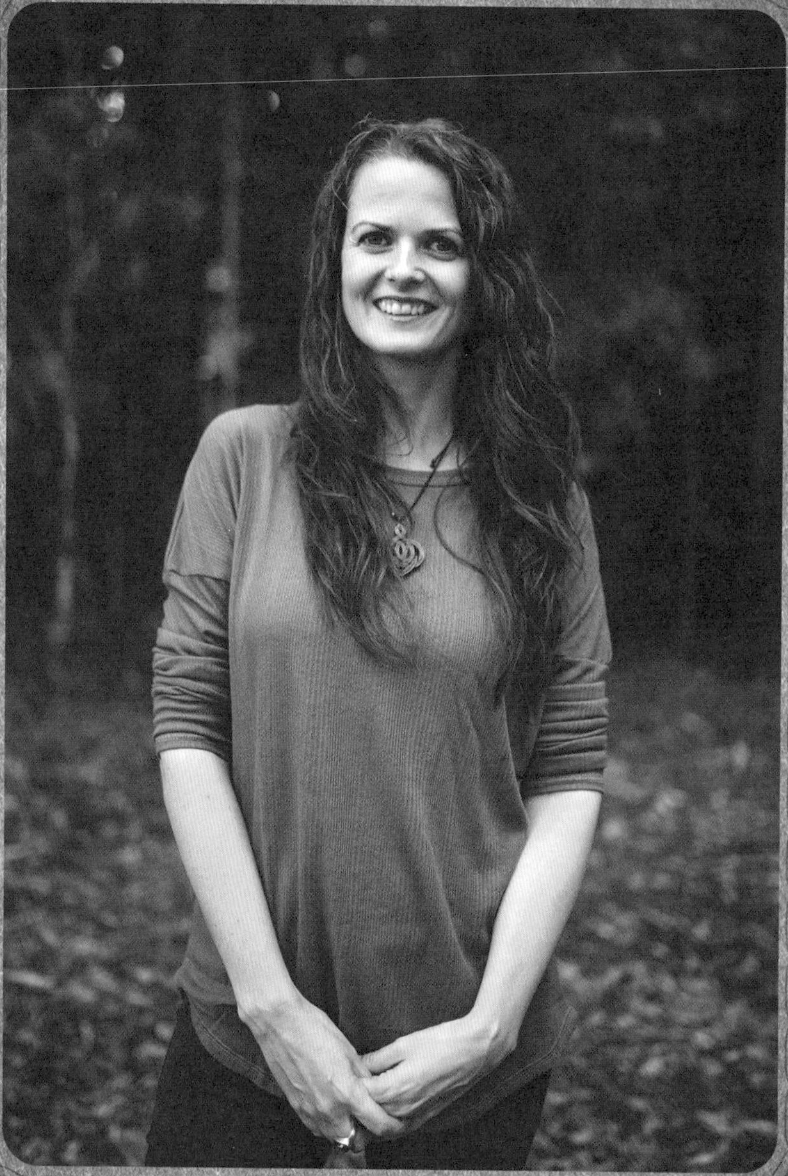

About the Author

Nicola McIntosh is a Western and Chinese herbalist and the author of *Plant Spirit Medicine* (Rockpool, 2022). She is also an artist and practises Celtic shamanism, which gives her a passion for everything nature related and the ability to see how ancient practices through modern applications can play an important role in our spiritual growth.

Nicola sees herself as a messenger for the spiritual realm, and through her work she aims to bring people from all walks of life together for a common goal. Her work allows you to look within to become your own teacher. She values the importance of self-care and her work is dedicated to raising consciousness through working on yourself and connecting more fully to nature, for the greater good.

WWW.SPIRITSTONE.COM.AU